TO:
Fowler,
Thanks for your contributions to this book. Hope you enjoy reliving the memories!

Best wishes,

Fred Kroner

"A SAUCER COMING TO REST"
A Half Century of the Assembly Hall

By Fred Kroner
with Melissa Merli

The News-Gazette®

Editor and Publisher
John Foreman

Project Editor
Amy George

Photo Editor
Darrell Hoemann

Art Director
Joan Millis

Cover design and book layout
Joan Millis, The News-Gazette

Hard cover ISBN: 978-0-9846063-6-8

Printed in the United States of America

The News-Gazette, Inc.
15 Main Street
Champaign, IL 61820
Phone: (217) 351-5252
Fax: (217) 351-5245
www.news-gazette.com

DEDICATION

For 16 consecutive summers, Danville's Mike Hulvey and Scott Eisenhauer have joined forces with Danville Area Community College to conduct the Sports Media Camp for Kids. It is a six-day interactive camp that leaves veteran journalists wondering, "Where was that when I was their age?"

The capable staff also includes R.J. Crace, Greg Doland, Andrew Harby, Logan Lee, Kaine Walters, Eric Westfall, Anthony Wilder and Rob Witzel.

This book is dedicated to the instructors who donate their time, and to the following 2012 campers who received the message: "Pursue your dreams. They are attainable."

Jordan Anderson, Paxton, Ill.
Ross Brown, Gibson City, Ill.
Andy Bunton, Danville, Ill.
Mitchell Day, Danville, Ill.
Jackson Evans, Shelburne, Vt.
Michael Gill, Danville, Ill.
Matthew Gocken, Indianola, Ill.
Caleb Griffin, Danville, Ill.
Cameron Griffin, Danville, Ill.
Damon Hays, Catlin, Ill.
Easton Hoskins, Georgetown, Ill.
Zach Kietzmann, Mahomet, Ill.
Caleb Medina, Danville, Ill.
Ryan Miller, Philo, Ill.
Jude Rayburn, Danville, Ill.
Jacob Stark, Chrisman, Ill.
Luke Steiner, Danville, Ill.
Caleb Trotter, Mahomet, Ill.
Isaac Trotter, Mahomet, Ill.
Landon Turner, Oakwood, Ill.
Liam White, Oakwood, Ill.

SPECIAL ACKNOWLEDGMENTS

Many behind-the-scenes persons deserve recognition for their valuable contributions to the project.

A heartfelt thanks goes to many of my *News-Gazette* colleagues, particularly John Foreman, Amy George, Joan Millis, Jim Rossow, Melissa Merli, Loren Tate, Jim Sollars and Darrell Hoemann.

From the Assembly Hall staff, a special and significant thank you goes out to Kevin Ullestad, Jennifer Larson, Janet Snyder, Tom Divan, Rose Munds and Sue Lyman.

Thanks are also in order to Dick Foley and Curt Beamer, who went above and beyond the call of duty with their assistance.

The News-Gazette's archives were also instrumental in tracking down a portion of the early Assembly Hall history.

ABOUT THE AUTHORS

Fred Kroner has worked for daily newspapers for 35 years, the first three at the Bloomington (Ill.) *Pantagraph* and the last 32 at *The News-Gazette*. He is the newspaper's prep sports coordinator.

This is his fourth book. The first was *Citizen Pain* (2001) about NBA player Brian Cardinal, who grew up in Tolono. The next was *Are You Ready?* (2007), about former University of Illinois public address announcer Jim Sheppard. The third book was *Catching Up* (2010), about the first 75 years of the amateur Eastern Illinois Baseball League.

Mr. Kroner was inducted into the Illinois Basketball Coaches Association Hall of Fame in 2009. He was recognized by the National Sportswriters and Sportscasters Association as Illinois Newsman of the Year in 2001. Four times, he was chosen as Newsman of the Year by the Illinois Wrestling Coaches and Officials Association (1987, 1988, 2000 and 2009). In 2010, he was chosen by the state's high school softball coaches as Newsman of the Year.

Kroner and his wife, Emily, live in Mahomet. Between the two of them, they have four children: Devin (Elizabeth) Kroner, Sal (Shea) Belahi, Jamel Belahi and Malika Belahi, as well as one grandson, Titus Kroner. who was born Nov. 17, 2012.

Melissa Merli has worked for daily newspapers since 1976, starting as the first woman to be hired as a full-time photographer at The Commercial-News in Danville. She eventually became a reporter and now covers the arts, entertainment and other topics for The News-Gazette. She graduated from the University of Illinois with a bachelor's degree in psychology and lives in Urbana.

CONTENTS

Introduction

"A Saucer Coming to Rest"

Buildings don't talk, but people do.

In the 50-year existence of the University of Illinois Assembly Hall, millions of words have been spoken and written about the unique 12-story-high structure that graces a 39-acre tract of land just south of Kirby Avenue in Champaign. Descriptions range from a modern marvel, to a giant mushroom, to a saucer on the horizon, to an inverted soup bowl.

The roof itself covers almost $4^1/_2$ acres. There's enough concrete to pave 71 miles of sidewalk. There's enough glass that if it were stretched out in one sheet, it would nearly match the 1,454-foot height of the Empire State Building.

It is the home court of the University of Illinois men's and women's basketball teams, the site of the IHSA wrestling tournament, the former home of the IHSA girls' and boys' basketball state tournaments and a venue where thousands of non-sports fans flock annually for concerts, conventions, graduations and theatrical productions. In addition, the interior has twice been used in movies. The first was in 1978 for the CBS made-for-TV movie about boxing, *Flesh and Blood*, for which it was transformed to play the roles of the Las Vegas Convention Center and New York's Madison Square Garden. The second was for the critically-acclaimed 1994 documentary *Hoop Dreams*, for which it was undisguised. In October 1982, it even served as the site for an indoor rodeo and the concrete floor was covered with eight inches of dirt.

In September 1958, Aberdeen Angus cattle were grazing on land owned by the UI and known as the School of Agriculture's north pasture. Kirby Avenue, near the Neil Street interchange a few blocks to the west, did not have a viaduct as wide or as tall as it became after much of the 110,000 cubic yards of dirt removed from the Assembly Hall hole was transported that short distance.

The person who drew up the building plans was 1929 UI architecture graduate Max Abramovitz whose credits already included work at the United Nations buildings, the Rockefeller Center and a majestic building at the Lincoln Center for the Performing Arts in New York. The U.N. was designed by a committee with Abramovitz serving as the architect in charge. His future credits would include the U.S. Steel Tower in Pittsburgh, as well as two other structures at his alma mater — the Krannert Center for the Performing Arts and the Hillel Foundation building.

In a 1957 newspaper interview about the design, Abramovitz told *The News-Gazette* the look would be similar to "a saucer coming to rest." His comments prompted a cartoon by Mel Sample, of Champaign. The drawing depicts two Martians standing in front of the completed structure. Both have doubts about what they see. Finally, one Martian says to his comrade, "They'll never get it off the ground."

The UI Board of Trustees gave their approval of the plans to construct the Assembly Hall on December 17, 1957. In an article in *The News-Gazette* the next day, it was noted that "an area east of the new structure is being reserved as the possible site of a new gymnasium in the indefinite future."

In October 1998, the Ubben Center opened at 1700 S. Fourth Street, Champaign — directly east of the Assembly Hall. It houses administrative offices as well as practice courts for the men's and women's basketball teams.

Excavation at the Assembly Hall project site began on May 26, 1959. The milestone beginning was marked with little fanfare. There was not even a ceremonial groundbreaking with local dignitaries on hand sporting shovels and hard hats. In fact, construction workers at the site didn't even wear hard hats.

At its opening, the Assembly Hall was the largest unsupported dome in the world and was described in newspaper articles as "a dream of the 21st century." The popular topic of conversation in the early 1960s was whether the building was structurally sound. One person whose opinion received national attention was acclaimed psychic Jeane Dixon, who predicted the Assembly Hall — which doesn't have a single steel beam or any interior supports — would collapse.

The Assembly Hall not only held strong, but also gained so much worldwide fanfare that in June 2011, *Business Insider* ranked it among the 100 best venues in sports, placing it at number 31. It scored 9 out of 10 for architecture/ambiance/aesthetics.

At the time of completion, it was the largest structure of its kind ever built on a university campus.

Illinois' Seven Wonders of Engineering

STRUCTURE	LOCATION
Assembly Hall	Champaign
Dresden Nuclear Power Station	Morris
Central District Filtration Plant	Chicago
AT&T Communications Switching Center	Norway
Chicago Area Expressway System	Chicago
Crab Orchard Resevoir Development	Carbondale
Sewarage and Sewage Treatment Facilities	Chicago

Source: Illinois Society of Professional Engineers, February 1964.

The building was one of seven nationwide nominated for the 1963 American Society of Civil Engineers' Outstanding Civil Engineering Achievement of the Year award (which was won by the Ohio River Valley Clean Streams Program).

Less than a year after the grand opening, the Illinois Society of Professional Engineers chose the Assembly Hall as first among the seven wonders of engineering in the state. It was the only building on the list. In its February 1964 release, the society said, "The Assembly Hall is a magnificent example of the joint product of many phases of engineering — structural, electrical, mechanical and architectural."

Three years later, another honor was bestowed on the Assembly Hall. A book entitled *The Elegant Solution* listed the structure as one of the six "most exciting breakthroughs of our time." The November 1967 publication detailing "the newest wonders of the world" was authored by Jean Ford Brennan, who noted that "the Assembly Hall is an exciting illustration of what can be done with concrete and imagination."

The Assembly Hall, which is eligible to be placed on the National Register of Historic Places, ranked number 3 in importance in a 1994 campus historic preservation plan (behind Altgeld Hall and Follenger Auditorium).

"It was the first building with a free-floating dome. Architecturally, they were able to do something no one else had done," former Illini basketball coach Bruce Weber says, "and that led to a lot of other successful buildings."

In 2013, the Assembly Hall may not technically be a "modern marvel" any longer, but without question, it is still a marvel in our modern world.

Don't take our word for it. How about the impressions of the person who coached more basketball games (321) and won more games (256) at the Assembly Hall than any other man?

Milestone Moments

EVENT	DATE	CROWD
Open house	March 2, 1963	39,317
First basketball game	March 4, 1963	17,137
First standing ovation (for Harry Belafonte)	October 31, 1964	6,296
First movie usage (*Flesh and Blood*)	December 3-6, 1978	1,000 extras hired
First stage show ("Desire Under the Elms")	October 29-30, 1964	Not available

"We loved it then, and still do," Lou Henson says. "It's unique. I don't know of another dome-shaped facility that looks like that. From the exterior, it's the most beautiful building I know of. On the inside, it is certainly a great facility."

It became even better during the Henson Era (1975-1996). "We originated the Orange Krush," Henson recalls. "With them on the floor, the enthusiasm gets going. I enjoyed playing there . . . I'll tell you one thing, with the crowds we have, there was all kinds of noise."

Count Henson among the throngs pleased that the Assembly Hall will be refurbished rather than destroyed shortly after its 50th birthday. "I'm happy, and I think everybody else is happy," Henson says. "Some seats in C [section] are quite a ways away, but they are at any facility. A lot of people would be very disappointed if they didn't continue to use it."

Some interior renovations were done during Henson's watch, such as the widening of the tunnel, but he knows there's more to be accomplished. "I'm sure there are things it needs, like air conditioning," he says.

It took approximately 23 months for one million visitors to pass through the Assembly Hall. The milestone mark was hit February 16, 1965, when 8,751 persons showed up for an Illini basketball win, 95-72, against Ohio State. That day's turnout pushed the total attendance at the new building to 1,003,802.

Assembly Hall director Tom Parkinson said the figures represented "organized crowds," or paid attendance, and did not account for the thousands of individuals who came to tour the facility when there were no events scheduled. First-year records revealed that visitors not only came from throughout the United States, but also from such foreign lands as Pakistan and Ireland.

For the first fiscal year, financial figures showed income from student service fees at $827,787 with expenses at $657,731. Income from events sponsored at the Assembly Hall was $249,510, which was greater than the amount paid for those events ($167,303).

Attendance Milestones

2 years	Winter 1965	1,000,000
5 years	Spring 1968	2,298,908
10 years	Spring 1973	5,000,000
15 years	Spring 1977	7,700,000
20 years	Spring 1983	11,255,268

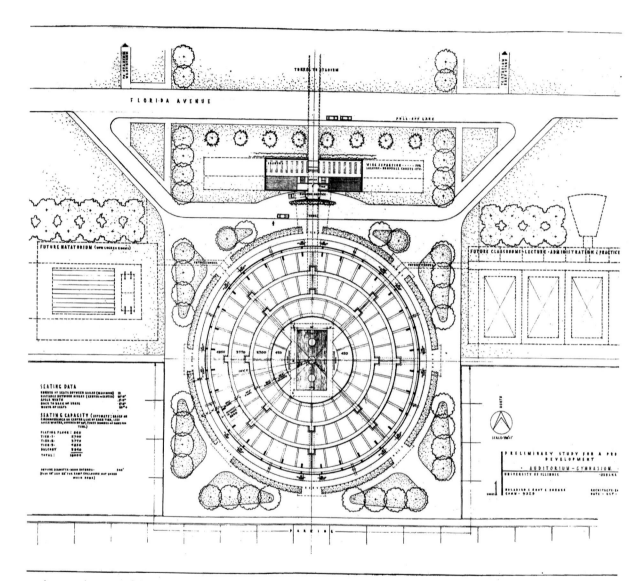

Architect's drawing of the Assembly Hall. Photo courtesy of the Assembly Hall.

PART I
BUILDING THE HALL

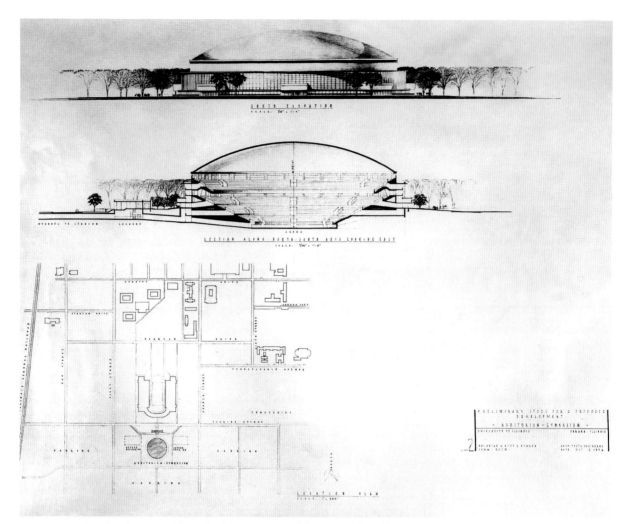

Preliminary plans for the Assembly Hall. Photo courtesy of the Assembly Hall.

Model of the Assembly Hall. Photo courtesy of the Assembly Hall.

1
Not Your Average Building

Developing plans for a new facility

The actual date when workers started at the Assembly Hall site is long after the project was first proposed. In 1941, University of Illinois officials had plans drawn up for a field house. A feasibility study suggested a site east of Huff Gymnasium, but that land was deemed more valuable for classroom space because it was so close to the UI library.

In 1945, the state granted an appropriation of $2 million for a facility that newspaper reporters dubbed "a sports palace." The lowest bid, however, came in $1 million above the appropriation. Work was never started on a building, which was also going to include a swimming pool, at a site just north of Memorial Stadium. By the time materials were available in 1947, the cost, including labor, had risen to nearly $4.2 million. Even when cuts were made, such as dropping the number of arena seats from 18,000 to 15,000, the price tag was budgeted at an unacceptable $3.3 million. The appropriation lapsed due to the budget, but the interest did not.

Champaign's R.A. Stipes was one of the ardent supporters. He was quoted in a 1945 *Champaign-Urbana Courier* article, saying "At present, gymnasium space is far less than that which is necessary in a normal year. Construction of the new building is a definite need early in the post-war period." At this time, enrollment at the UI was about 8,500. A decade later, the number of students on campus had more than doubled, rising to 18,075. As the end of the 1956 calendar year approached, Illinois was the only Big Ten Conference member without a field house. Some universities already had two.

The University of Illinois, however, had a new president, Dr. David Dodds Henry, who had more than a cursory interest in upgraded athletic facilities. Before the spring semester of the 1956-57 school year was over, New York architect Max Abramovitz was on campus to start formulating plans for a combination auditorium and gymnasium. His firm, Harrison and Abramovitz, was given six months to develop the blueprint. The location picked was south of Memorial Stadium.

Even at such an early stage in the process, newspaper archives (*News-Gazette*, April 1957) reveal one thought of Abramovitz's that was never scrapped: "There are advantages to walking in at ground level, with steps down and steps up." Abramovitz also said the building would be a "real piece of architecture work, not a freak," and he envisioned seating for 18,000-20,000 persons.

Senator E.R. Peters (R-St. Joseph) sponsored legislation for the building to be financed through student fees. Quoted in *The News-Gazette*, Peters said "I hope that we might get a state appropriation for a part of the cost, so as to keep the student fees as low as possible. . . . If the only method is to charge fees from students, then I'll do everything I can to get the necessary bills through the legislature." Ultimately, no taxpayer dollars were ever used for the building or its maintenance.

In April 1959, the UI Board of Trustees gave their consent to build on land that was used as overflow parking during the UI football season. A month later, the former pasture was turned into a construction site. UI athletic director Douglas R. Mills, a former Illini basketball player and head coach (of the famed Whiz Kids), was outspoken in his views for a basketball building from the time he took over as the AD in 1941. When his dream came to fruition, he could hardly contain his elation. "For years now, we have been the most inadequate school in the middle west for basketball facilities," Mills told *News-Gazette* sports editor Bill Schrader in April 1959. "This isn't a distinction one likes to have. Now we'll be on top."

Mills was so optimistic that he publicly predicted the Illini would play their 1960-61 basketball season in the Assembly Hall. That proved overly optimistic, but there was truth in another of his contentions. It was a boon for coach Harry Combes as he hit the recruiting trail. "When you are talking to boys about playing in a structure like the Assembly Hall instead of Huff Gymnasium, they listen a little better," Mills said. "Other schools were using the Assembly Hall as a weapon against us. . . . They were telling the ball players it would never be built, that this was just propaganda we were putting out. Now they can read it for themselves. They can see that they will really have the opportunity to play in the finest building in the world. People from all over the world are going to come and look at this building."

One high school standout who was enticed to the UI was Canton's Dave Downey, who still holds the Illini's single-game scoring record (53 points), and he brought along good friend Bill Small.

"When we were being recruited, the Assembly Hall had been committed to," Downey recalls. "They said we would play in it when we were sophomores." Downey and Small wound up playing only the final two home games of their senior year at the Assembly Hall.

Construction plans generate objections

Seldom is there total satisfaction. Not even a world-renowned architect could please everyone with a building that became the University of Illinois Assembly Hall. There were naysayers who didn't want the Assembly Hall to be built. Some wanted the money directed to academic-focused structures or to improve salaries of the professors.

In outlining their opposition in a *News-Gazette* article on May 31, 1958, the Urbana chapter of the American Association of University Professors cited several objections. "Our present general view regarding the proposed assembly hall is that the building should be cancelled and the $5 million of funds available from the same source used for the construction of additional intramural athletic facilities — including perhaps an outdoor swimming pool — to promote general physical fitness, and a moderate-sized auditorium to promote cultural development. In the area of sports facilities, we feel the emphasis should be placed on participant sports rather than spectator sports," said William H. McPherson, president of the AAUP Urbana chapter.

"Athletic director (Douglas) Mills refers to the declining spirit or interest in the team. He attributes this to the fact that students can attend only four games a year and suggests that the spirit will mount when they can attend all of the games. On these views, we hold a contrary view. The declining interest seems to us a long-term trend largely unrelated to spectacular facilities. And of course we do not concur in the premise that an increase in student enthusiasm for the team is in itself a worthwhile goal. On the contrary, we consider it fortunate that the students' loyalty to and pride in their university is coming to be based increasingly on considerations other than the athletic prowess of a few students.

Abramovitz at the UI Krannert Center, 1968. Photo courtesy of The Assembly Hall.

"While the structure would be well-suited to the spring tournament, it seems anomalous for the University to encourage thousands of high school students to absent themselves from their classes several days at a time when we are emphasizing that the schools must give more thorough training to prospective university students."

Prior to this, a *Chicago Daily News* editorial in December 1957 opposed the Assembly Hall project. The editorial staff alluded to the advance publicity that indicated there would be no obstructed views in the building "when a 7-foot center working for his scholarship puts a ball through the hoop. To hike (student) fees for the purpose of wrapping a basketball court in luxury is surely questionable procedure in this year of Sputniks I and II. The trustees did not see fit to raise student fees in order to raise salaries, evidently concluding that the faculty pay was a matter for the taxpayers to shoulder. But they see nothing wrong in increasing the cost of a student's year at Champaign-Urbana by $40 in order to build non-academic facilities. . . . Students who go to the University of Illinois to get an education, rather than to watch basketball games, have just cause for indignation."

About the architect

Maxwell Abramovitz was born in Chicago in May 1908, the son of Romanian Jewish immigrants Benjamin and Sophia (Maimon) Abramovitz. He graduated from Crane High School in 1924 and spent part of a year in the banking industry before enrolling in college. He was 21 when he earned his bachelor's degree in architectural engineering from the University of Illinois in 1929.

He remained at the UI for a year thereafter as a teaching assistant and then spent a year in Paris. By 1931, he was at Columbia University teaching architecture. By the end of the 1930s, he was an associate professor at Yale.

During WWII, he enlisted and became a Lieutenant Colonel with the United States Army Corps of Engineers. He received a Legion of Merit Award in 1945 for his service in China, where he built air fields.

His work can be seen in 11 states, as well as in Havana, Cuba, and Rio De Janeiro, Brazil, two locations where he designed U.S. embassies. Abramovitz was also responsible for the Central Intelligence Agency headquarters at Langley, Virginia, as well as two structures in Paris. He designed corpo-

Max Abramovitz. Photo courtesy of *The News-Gazette.*

rate structures as well as religious chapels. He not only drew up cultural buildings, but also military facilities.

Two years before the UI Assembly Hall opened, he was interviewed by Roger Ebert — who was then a staff writer for *The News-Gazette* — and said the building "will be the most exciting ... the best thing ... I've ever worked on." He continued, "Every part is alive, vital, functional. If everything goes just right, this building will represent the ideal I've always been shooting for. I really believe it. Every time I see it, I get the feeling it's coming closest to my idea of what a building ought to be."

Six months before the Assembly Hall was finished, a building which many consider Abramovitz's greatest professional achievement opened: the Philharmonic Hall at the Lincoln Center for the Performing Arts in New York. First Lady Jacqueline Kennedy attended the September 1962 premier.

He worked on it concurrently to the Assembly Hall project. Abramovitz actually started the $15.4 million Philharmonic Hall (now called Avery Fisher Hall) later, but the building was completed sooner.

Abramovitz was two months from his 55th birthday when the Assembly Hall was unveiled at its official grand opening. Abramovitz and his first wife, Anne Marie, had two children, a son and a daughter. In addition to his teachings and his designs, he was the author of two books.

Locally, Abramovitz's talents are evidenced at the $21 million Krannert Center for the Performing Arts (which opened on April 19, 1969) and also at the Hillel Foundation building on the UI campus.

The architect held a special place in his heart for his collegiate alma mater. "If it is felt that I have succeeded somewhat in my field, I must admit that I owe much to this University, where I have always felt the warmth and hospitality of this environment, an environment which encourages the concept that an individual and his aspirations are of vital interest to our society and to his fellow man," he told *News-Gazette* staff writer Fran Myers. "It is my hope that where I began my studies, we can continue to give this environment to all, no matter what discipline, so that our society can have the desire to understand, the ability to express and the talent to produce something worthwhile for us today, as well as contribute to the future."

Illini fans like to consider the Assembly Hall a one-of-a-kind structure, but Abramovitz had one model to use in reference as he drew up the blue prints. In advance of the 1960 Rome Olympics, that community unveiled a $424,000 domed sports palace, Palazzetto dello Sport. Fifty five years after its opening, the 5,000-seat facility is still in use.

According to *News-Gazette* sports writer Bill Schrader, Abramovitz visited the building, which is 194 feet in diameter (less than half the size of the Assembly Hall) and required 16 months to complete.

For much of his professional career, Abramovitz partnered with Wallace Harrison in the Harrison and Abramovitz firm. At the time of his death in September 2004, at age 96, he was living in Pound Ridge, New York. He was survived by his son and daughter along with five grandchildren.

He was a self-described workaholic who was quoted in a *New York Times* story in 2004 as saying, "I sit, relax, read a little and start over again. I'm just a working fool."

2
Construction Begins

Dick Foley had less than 24 hours to transition from one phase of his life to the next. He graduated from the University of Illinois on June 12, 1949. "The next day I went to work at Felmley Dickerson Co.," Foley recalls. Less than a decade thereafter, Foley was the project manager for the largest building venture ever at his alma mater. His company was the low bidder for the construction of the Assembly Hall. Felmley Dickerson, an Urbana company, submitted its bid at $7,859,788, to build the structure. The breakdown was as follows:

General work	$5,060,041
Electrical work	1,075,500
Heating, ventilation	906,793
Site work	538,093
Plumbing	259,000
Elevator	16,191
Sprinkler	4,170
TOTAL	$7,859,788

Six companies (listed below) submitted bids to construct the Assembly Hall. According to published newspaper reports, other companies were discouraged from submitting bids because they weren't convinced the design would work.

COMPANY	BID
Felmley Dickerson Co., Champaign-Urbana	$7,859,788
Corbetta Construction Co., Chicago	$8,023,000
Perini Corp., Framingham, Mass.	$8,998,000
Wm. E. Schweitzwer and Co., Evanston, Ill.	$9,123,000
O.W. Burke Co., Detroit	$9,170,000
Johnson, Drake and Piper, Inc., Terre Haute, Ind.	$9,765,248

The University of Illinois Board of Trustees approved the budget to the lowest bidder and awarded the contract to Felmley Dickerson Co. on May 16, 1959, after reworking for cutbacks, as follows:

ITEM	AMOUNT
Building construction	$6,457,292
Architectural, engineering services	500,535
Equipment (not seating)	373,700
Administrative costs	268,410
Contingency	116,063
University work	34,000
TOTAL	$7,750,000

Foley was young enough and naive enough to not get flustered by the enormous challenge. "You think you can handle everything," Foley says, "and you're not intimidated at the beginning; maybe after you get into it."

Ray Dickerson was president of the company. "He put the bid together and designed the form system for the roof," Foley says.

Ed Maliskas was the project superintendant and Ed Skoog was the engineer. "[Skoog's] job was to get the dimensions right, including the level of the roof," Foley recalls. The uniqueness of the building meant there weren't other models to follow. They were trendsetters from the beginning.

"I thought it would be difficult," Foley says. "Most buildings are rectangular or square, not a circle. It was one-of-a-kind and because it was so much different, it was difficult."

They started at the ground level. "You had to figure how to get in and out of the place," Foley recounts. "How do you work inside and have access to the outside?" Foley and the hundreds of other construction workers were there to follow a predetermined plan, the drawing of another UI graduate, architect Max Abramovitz. "The architect designed it, so you build what they design," Foley says. "The chances of making any suggestions are nil. He was very strict as far as seeing it done exactly as it was designed. I think we let the architect dominate us a little bit."

The groundbreaking occurred in May 1959. The original timetable called for completion by July 1961, but the work was actually completed in February 1963. "It took longer than anybody expected," Foley recalls. "We had 19 weeks of labor strikes the first year. When we were finally done, after all that time, it was 'whew.'"

A four-month steel strike, which began in late August 1959, slowed progress, as did a two-week strike of operating engineers. Then, in 1962, about 80 cement masons and 30 plasterers went on strike. Plasterers had asked for a 15-cent raise from their base pay ($3.90) for each of two years on a new contract, but were only offered a $12\frac{1}{2}$-cent raise. The cement masons did not publically announce how much of a raise they were seeking from their base pay ($3.60). Their work stoppages, combined, lasted 40 weeks.

The timing of the strikes, and the ensuing delays, proved more costly than just the lost hours on the job. "You can't build the roof in the winter time," Foley says. "You had to be in position to do that in the spring and summer. The summer strike cost us a year." The delays meant little chance of profit for the Felmley Dickerson Co. "We lost money, instead of making money," Foley says. "It lasted 4 years when we'd figured $2\frac{1}{2}$ years. This was our contribution to the University."

An advance estimate of man hours needed by individuals in the various construction trades was as follows:

Common laborers	123,000
Carpenters	82,000
Ironworkers	40,000
Concrete finishers	20,000
Operators	19,000
Teamsters	10,000
Masons	3,000

Completion of the Assembly Hall was both rewarding and a letdown for Foley. "To be part of something like this is really almost a culmination of a career," Foley says, "and we finished it when I was 38. I had 25 more years to work. . . . After this job, you think that's what you ought to do all the time. It was harder to be challenged. It caused me to think more about treating our contractors well. What it did was make it harder to satisfy the owners for other jobs you didn't have the desire to do."

Felmley Dickerson Co.'s multitude of other credits included work at the former Chanute Air Force Base in Rantoul; J.M. Jones in Urbana; Quaker Oats in Danville, and for Carle Foundation Hospital and Carle Clinic in Urbana. "We probably worked in 30 towns," Foley says. "We went to Quincy once to build a hospital. The idea was we'd do whatever building construction work there was in Central Illinois."

Foley takes pride in more than the way the building has held up over the first five decades. The dome-shaped roof — which weighs approximately 8,640,000 pounds, or 4,320 tons — was kept in place by a process in which 614 miles of quarter-inch wire was tightened around the structure. The roof consists of 24 leaves, or folded-plate dome sections, that each weigh 170 pounds per foot and are 15 degrees wide. "Normal concrete weighs 4,000 pounds per cubic yard," Foley says. "This was special. It weighed 3,000 pounds per cubic yard."

To finish the concrete work on the roof required about three months with 50 laborers, carpenters and cement workers on the job. The material on the ceiling is called insulrock. It is both an insulating material and an acoustical material.

Subcontractors for Work on the Hall

Potter Electric Service Inc., Urbana	Electric service
R.H. Bishop Co., Champaign	Heating
R. Hays Co., Champaign	Plumbing
Builder's Supply, Champaign	Concrete
Illiana Construction Co., Urbana	Outside utilities
Bacon & Van Buskirk, Champaign	Windows

February 20, 1961. Photo courtesy of the Assembly Hall.

Photo courtesy of the Champaign County Historical Archives, The Urbana Free Library, Urbana, Illinois.

June 20, 1961. Photo courtesy of the Assembly Hall.

The first roof segment poured was along the southwest rim and the second was along the northeast rim. "To keep it balanced," Foley says, "we had to pour opposite slabs." The process was a time-consuming one. Concrete was hoisted from ground level by a boom crane with each bucket carrying less than one cubic yard. Each segment has three valleys at the bottom, but narrows to one valley near the top. The wire was wrapped around the building 2,467 times in 44 vertical rows, each separated by steel bars.

"For a job like that, where you're up in the air, we were fortunate we never had any major injuries on the job," he says.

Materials used in construction

Concrete (4,150 truck loads)	20,700 cu. yards
Roof concrete	3,042 cu. yards
Steel (48 carloads)	2,370 tons
Lumber	820,000 board feet
Plywood	150,000 square feet
Dirt removal	187,000 cu. yards

Beginning in 2000, there was talk about the possibility of the Assembly Hall being torn down and replaced by another multi-purpose facility. For obvious reasons, Foley was opposed. "We want it to stay," he says. "We want to say we did something."

Reinforcing steel for roof slab, 1961. Photo by Gus Lundquist from the Dick Foley collection.

Temporary center tower, 1961. Photo by Gus Lundquist from the Dick Foley collection.

Raising the roof

Earthmoving equipment, provided by Feutz Construction Company of Paris, Illinois, removed 110,000 cubic yards of earth at the site. The interior excavation was not done until after the framework of the structure was finished. The hall is a concrete bowl sunk into the ground and reinforced, allowing it to be self-supporting. There are no interior posts or pillars, so every spectator has an unobstructed view.

A 30-foot wide concourse circles the outside of the seating area. Half of that space is broken up by the buttresses that create 48 niches. Inside, there are 47 rows of permanent seating. There are 13 in the lower section (A), 11 in the middle section (B) and 23 in the upper section (C). The top row alone features 1,000 seats.

Before work started on the roof, a 100-foot tower was erected inside the Assembly Hall. The concrete roof was poured in pie-shaped sections, 5 feet wide at the point and 25 feet wide at the outside. Originally envisioned as a smooth roof, it was subsequently changed to concrete corrugations for added strength.

A total of 614 miles of quarter-inch steel wire was wrapped around the rim (at 120,000 to 130,000 pounds per square inch) to post tension the girders. For comparison purposes, the amount of wire used is significantly more than the length of the state of Illinois, which is 395 miles long.

An eight-ton wire-winding machine tightened the cable. The tension on the cable caused the roof to lift, according to Felmley Dickerson project manager Dick Foley, "by $3^3/_4$ inches." The roof was already inside the bowl, sitting on the edge beam. The edge beam rests on the upper seat area. The wire was then wrapped. It took nine weeks to complete the wiring portion of the project.

The inside structure that provided the beam support — described by some as a spiderweb look — was dismantled and removed. The outer shell rests on 48 reinforced concrete buttresses.

Raising forms for pouring slab between center tower and 130 support tower, 1961. Photo by Gus Lundquist from the Dick Foley collection.

Pouring section of upper bowl and edge beam, 1960. Photo by Gus Lundquist from the Dick Foley collection.

Pouring a buttress in 1959. Photo by Gus Lundquist from the Dick Foley collection.

Glasswork

Depending on the definition of "big," the glasswork at the UI Assembly Hall might not qualify as the biggest project done by Bacon & Van Buskirk. "We did bigger jobs, dollar-wise, at hospitals, other buildings at the UI, at Eastern Illinois and at Southern Illinois," Roy Van Buskirk says, "but I don't know that we did anything as distinctive architecturally." When the building was in its infancy, Van Buskirk found the finished product hard to envision. "We looked at the drawings, but couldn't imagine how well it would turn out," he says.

Bacon & Van Buskirk installed 700 panes of glass, each weighing 200 pounds. Cecil Reed was in charge of the installation crew. He was joined on the site by Eddie Billman, Jim Johnson, Walter Moore and Donald Woods. Collectively, they put in what amounted to a quarter-mile of glass. The crew made certain that the materials were well-preserved; only one pane was dropped.

Van Buskirk remembers that the glass installation crew had a challenge not normally encountered. Because there's an inward slant to the Hall, when workers stood flush with the edge at the surface, their colleagues at the top (23 feet above) were 8 feet removed from the building, and thus away from the top of the glass panes (which are perfectly straight). "Vertical scaffolding couldn't reach the top," Van Buskirk recalls. "We had to figure a way to get the top person closer to the building than the guy on the bottom." Consultants from Chicago were summoned, Van Buskirk remembers. They provided several options and suggestions, but ultimately none of their advice was heeded. "The way we finally did it was as low-tech as possible," Van Buskirk says. The company constructed a special system that catered to the contour of the building. Essentially, two giant ladders were pieced together

Photo courtesy of the Champaign County Historical Archives, The Urbana Free Library, Urbana, Illinois.

and nestled into the scaffolding on either end. "Then we literally walked the glass up the ladder," Van Buskirk recalls. Van Buskirk's workers also faced another challenge: "A lot of the fill dirt had been put in, and in many places that required a lot of lifting to get to the bottom of the glass area," Van Buskirk says.

The glass was made in England and imported. "Mr. Abramovitz [the architect] had participated in the United Nations buildings where every country provided some kind of material," Van Buskirk says. "The square mesh wire [within the glass] was what the British provided. [Abramovitz] liked the pattern and that's what he specified." Knowing that the glass couldn't be produced in the United States, Van Buskirk made certain the architect knew there were other choices. "We gave him an alternate so the glass wouldn't have to be imported," Van Buskirk recalls, "but he wanted that design."

Figuring how much glass to order to complete the job wasn't difficult. The tougher call was determining how much additional glass was needed to account for breakage or future replacements. "We ordered 20 percent extra," Van Buskirk related. "It turns out we didn't need it, and we eventually used it in other places."

Van Buskirk is pleased to have left his stamp on the building where hundreds of workers were contributors. "We really took a lot of pride in it," he says, "as did the guys who worked in the other trades."

Roy Van Buskirk, in his early 30s when the Assembly Hall was built, became the second generation owner of Bacon & Van Buskirk. His father, Verne, who died in 1970, formed the business in 1937. Roy's son, Rodney, runs the company as the 50-year anniversary of the Assembly Hall approaches.

15

Photo courtesy of the Champaign County Historical Archives, The Urbana Free Library, Urbana, Illinois.

Partial roof slabs, 1961. Photo by Gus Lundquist from the Dick Foley collection.

Financing the build

Financing was handled through a loan with interest rates on the self-liquidating bonds of approximately $2^{1}/_{2}$ percent throughout the construction period, and $4^{3}/_{4}$ percent thereafter. The note was retired in 1984, paid for through student fees and proceeds of events hosted at the Assembly Hall.

Students had voted by a 4-to-1 margin in favor of the student fee for Assembly Hall construction in 1958. However, by the time the Assembly Hall opened in 1963, most of those individuals were no longer on campus.

The money for the Assembly Hall was part of a four-building package totaling more than $14,500,000, an appropriation that was the second largest ever received by the university. This package included $5 million for an addition on the south side of the Illini Union (which was opened in 1941), $1.15 million for the Student Services Building and $850,000 for an addition to McKinley Hospital.

The $7.75 million dollar contract was increased to $8.3 million when the Board of Trustees approved the sale of an additional $600,000 in revenue bonds on February 20, 1962. Among the major changes to the design was a service entrance at the north end of the Assembly Hall that permitted vehicles to drive down a ramp and unload equipment or materials directly onto the activity floor.

The previous plans called for an elevator system to be in place. That plan was not totally scrapped — a freight elevator was retained. In addition, a permanent maple floor surface was replaced by a terrazzo-like surface (a Kalman floor) that could accommodate a greater variety of events. A portable maple floor (divided into 225 panel sections) is put down when needed for basketball games. It is raised seven inches above the concrete floor. The actual floor space is 88 feet by 140; the basketball court takes up only 59.8 feet by 120 feet.

Ultimately, the Assembly Hall price tag ended up at $8.5 million.

Neoprene expansion joint between window wall and concrete seating area, 1962. Photo by Gus Lundquist from the Dick Foley collection.

Assembly Hall Statistics

Circumference	1,250 feet
Diameter	400 feet
Height	125 feet
Floor	24 feet below ground level
Furthest seat	185 feet from center court
Roof's weight	8,640,000 million pounds
Roof's size	125,663 square feet
Shell roof	varies from 3 feet, 6 inches to 7 feet, 6 inches in thickness
Permanent seating	16,128 (at opening)
2012 capacity	16,618 (for basketball)
Glass	35,000 square feet
Glass (weight)	140,000 pounds

Photos courtesy of The Assembly Hall.

Aerial view of the Assembly Hall with Memorial Stadium. Photo courtesy of the Assembly Hall.

3
Settling on a Name

What do you call a one-of-a-kind structure that serves many purposes? It hosts basketball games and the state high school sporting events, as well as concerts, conventions, graduations, plays, circuses, ice events and monster truck shows.

"The Assembly Hall" was the tag former president Dr. David Dodds Henry coined simply as a working title. From the outset, Henry wanted to avoid words such as "gymnasium" and "arena" in the title because those terms are more closely associated with sports, and he envisioned the building as one with multiple functions.

The Assembly Hall name stuck, though not without considerable debate. No issue was more discussed — or cussed — than what to call the circular structure on the southern portion of the UI campus.

A 1963 ballot was put out to students to determine their non-binding hopes. Students were asked to cast one vote in Column A and one vote in Column B.

COLUMN A
___ Max Abramovitz
___ John Bardeen
___ Avery Brundage
___ Stephen A. Douglas
___ Harold "Red" Grange
___ Ernest Hemingway
___ Illini
___ Edmund Janes James
___ Lloyd Morey
___ Alan Nevins
___ James "Scotty" Reston
___ Carl Sandburg
___ Frederick Seitz
___ Adlai Stevenson
___ Robert Zuppke

COLUMN B
___ Assembly Hall
___ Memorial Assembly Hall
___ Arena
___ Amphitheatre
___ Coliseum
___ Hall

For those so inclined, there were two additional possibilities Assembly Hall (without a proper name to serve as a prefix) and a write-in option.

A total of 13,057 ballots were cast in the special student referendum, which took place during registration for the spring 1963 semester. UI student senator John Lundtsen released the results, which showed two clear-cut favorites among the top four:

RANK, NAME	VOTES
1. Zuppke Hall	2,999
2. Illini Hall	2,837
3. Carl Sandburg	1,930
4. Harold "Red" Grange	1,645

Some of the numerous write-in suggestions included:

Overpriced Abortion
Illium
Illititium
Ping Pong Palace
Pleasure Palace
Circus Maximus
Cuspidor Hall
John Wilkes Booth Memorial Assembly Hall
Corn Bowl
Dirksen Hall

Frost Coliseum
The Cymbal
Huff Gym
Illini Folly
Max's Mistake
The Mushroom
The Hole
The Oyster
The $20 Raise in Tuition Building

The student sentiments were forwarded to the UI Board of Trustees, which holds the power to name any campus building. They took no action. Trustees addressed the issue at a regularly-scheduled meeting two weeks after the grand opening. Speaking to a *Champaign-Urbana Courier* reporter, Wayne Johnston said, "We named it Assembly Hall [in 1959]. I think we ought to let it rock along for awhile and see what is made of the hall."

His colleagues saw value in the publicity that had already been generated for the Assembly Hall moniker and took note of the favorable reactions. They also favored functional names as opposed to individual names in the titling of a building. The group indicated that the "no action" decision was not irrevocable and could be revisited at a future time.

Speculation swirled that Zuppke's high rank was partially based on an editorial in the student newspaper, the *Daily Illini*, published the previous December shortly before the first semester ended. The newspaper backed the Zuppke Hall name and urged the UI Student Senate to take action to start the process. Part of the sentiment was attributed to Zuppke's death on December 22, 1957, just five days after the Assembly Hall project was approved by the Board of Trustees.

One person who supported naming the Assembly Hall for Zuppke (the UI football head coach from 1913-1941), was All-American Harold "Red" Grange. Quoted in the *Daily Illini* in December, 1962, Grange said he "could think of no one more deserving of the honor."

UI president Dr. David Dodds Henry reminded trustees, "experience has indicated that names of buildings may be changed if there are sufficient reasons to warrant such action. As the functional uses of the Assembly Hall may develop in the future, the name selected first may need to be changed later."

Those who thought the naming issue had been resolved were dead wrong. Illinois governor Otto Kerner proposed a name change less than two weeks after President John F. Kennedy was assassinated on November 22, 1963.

In a letter to the Trustees, Kerner wrote: "As a tribute to the late President Kennedy, I request that, at the next meeting of the Board of Trustees of the University of Illinois, you consider naming the new Assembly Hall on the Champaign campus in his honor. . . . It is fitting and proper that this unique and magnificent structure bear the name of John F. Kennedy, because he brought to the presidency a love of athletics and the arts — two vital facets of our life for which the Assembly Hall was erected."

Board sentiment was split. Decatur's Harold Pogue, a democrat, backed Kerner's proposal. Republican member Earl Hughes, of Woodstock, was against it. In an interview with a *Champaign-Urbana Courier* reporter, Hughes said: "I certainly believe in appropriate memorials to the late President and other outstanding citizens, but I think appropriate action has been taken by the nation, and I would be opposed to changing the name of the Hall."

Pogue's feelings, he said, were based on Kennedy's commitment to physical fitness. "It would be a very fitting memorial because it does house sports, art and educational functions, all of which the late President was certainly an advocate of."

Odds were against the possibility from the outset. When the request was made, only one campus building (Lincoln Hall, erected in 1911) was named in honor of a past U.S. president, notably, one with strong Illinois ties.

The News-Gazette took the issue to the streets, interviewing 40 random subjects. Of those, 22 supported renaming the Assembly Hall, 14 were opposed and 4 were neutral. Following is a sampling of the opinions:

- "Yes. The Assembly Hall is a unique building and President Kennedy was a unique man," Mrs. W. Gordon Hunt, Champaign.
- "It doesn't make any difference, just so they don't move it," C.L. Lindsey, Urbana.
- "I would favor it, but if they don't give it a name, I'll still go," Wayne Eberhardt, Champaign.
- "With no disrespect to the late President, we are changing the names of too many things too fast," Bob Smith, Rantoul.
- "It's a fine idea to give respect to his memory, but everything completed near the time of his death shouldn't be given his name. We can go too far," Daniel Allison, Urbana.
- "I think it's a good idea. Perhaps if we are reminded of the man, we will remember his ideas," Julianne Blakley, Urbana.
- "President Kennedy was not a product of Illinois and there are many men who have done more for Illinois for whom the Assembly Hall could be named after," Tracey Luckey, Mattoon.
- "I suggest a wait of six months until some of the emotional strain wears off and then if the public still feels it should be named after the late President, I do not object," Rev. Donald Scott, Atwood.

Photo courtesy of the Assembly Hall.

- "I think it would be a great tribute, but I'm not sure people would call it by its new name. Everyone is so used to Assembly Hall," Mrs. H.I. Ingraham, Urbana.
- "It has gone long enough without a name and since he [President Kennedy] was the idol of young people and this being a building for young people, I think it would be a nice gesture," Mrs. E.E. Ferguson, Tuscola.
- "It would be appropriate if a name had not already been selected for the Assembly Hall, but I can't see changing a name which was been established," Mrs. Maxine Chapman, Atwood.

In its December 19, 1963, edition, the *Champaign-Urbana Courier* reported that letters to the editor were running "10 to 1 against Gov. Kerner's suggestion." Board of Trustee president Howard W. Clement, of Peoria, said those numbers didn't definitely reflect the prevailing opinion. "Letters are usually written by people objecting to something," Clement said. Letters to the Board of Trustees were overwhelmingly against Kerner's proposal to name the building for Kennedy.

More telling was another student referendum that was held in conjunction with Student Senate elections and released in February 1964. The preferences were as follows:

NAME	VOTES
UI Assembly Hall	1,187
John F. Kennedy Memorial Hall	806
Illini Assembly Hall	338
Robert Zuppke Assembly Hall	195
Red Grange Assembly Hall	94

Although the Assembly Hall was new, the concept of naming a campus building after a sitting president who died in office was not. In 1945, there were suggestions for renaming UI campus buildings in honor of Franklin D. Roosevelt, but no such changes were made.

Is the issue resolved? Will Assembly Hall be the official name forever? At least one person hopes not.

"I never liked the name," says Dave Downey, one of the Illini's all-time basketball greats. "I thought it should have been named something. Maybe now they can sell the naming rights to it."

The News-Gazette

FRIDAY, MARCH 1, 1963.   20 PAGES

UNVEIL GIANT ILLINI ASSEMBLY HALL!

Gala Events Start At 1:30 Saturday

By FRAN MYERS
News-Gazette University Editor

The University of Illinois' $6,350,000 Assembly Hall opens Saturday.

Thousands of persons are expected to be welcomed by University of Illinois students to the world-renowned Assembly Hall between 1:30 and 5 p. m. and 7:30 and 11 p. m. Saturday at a gala Open House.

The doors will be open to visitors to observe with the University its 95th birthday anniversary.

Although the Assembly Hall will not be fully completed and occupied by those groups to be located in the new structure, the building is in readiness to be seen by the general public.

Built without benefit of state tax funds, but through fees assessed students registered in the University and from I n c o m e from the Hall itself, the structure will stand dedicated to the Illini who have planned for it, who have worked upon the building, and who now will pay for the structure.

The Open House to which the University is inviting everybody will be followed by Illinois basketball games as the Illini play Northwestern at 8 p.m. Monday and Iowa at 8 p.m. March 9, as the opening ball games in the new Hall. The games are sold out.

Funds to construct the building were secured through bond issues of $8,- 330,000. The bonds run for 25 years.

Felmley-Dickerson Co., Urbana, of which Ray Dickerson is president, is the general contractor on the Assembly Hall.

University of Illinois students will serve as Illini Guides who will greet visitors at the doors and serve as hosts and hostesses throughout the building, to describe its features and talk to visitors. All will be welcomed to the concourse, the glass enclosed area; the office level and the principal auditorium of the new multi-purpose building.

Students also will present an afternoon entertainment at intervals.

Designed as a great multipurpose building by Max Abramovitz, of the firm of Harrison and Abramovitz, New York City, the Assembly Hall in its initial opening will be placed in use for various areas of entertainment. Music, military and athletic presentations characterize the initial programs for the Open House.

These events will be only the beginning of what is expected to attract international attention in the use of this uniquely designed structure.

The Assembly Hall will be formally dedicated at the time the University of Illinois honors its scholars and those who have achieved academic superiority, on Honors Day, May 3.

President David D. Henry of the University of Illinois often has referred to the Assembly Hall and to its uses as a place for recreational development. It is believed that as the Assembly Hall is placed in use there will be more and more events of an educational nature planned for the structure.

The Assembly Hall, built as two huge concrete bowls, placed face to face, one as the seat bowl and the other as the dome bowl, is adaptable for basketball with a portable floor which will be placed on top of the concrete floor. Also, it may be used for ice shows, with the ice show companies using a portable floor, and other athletic programs, such as gymnastic performances, fencing and other events. Also by use of a portable stage,

★ ★ ★ ★

ASSEMBLY HALL AT A GLANCE

WHERE: On 39 acre area, bounded on the north by Florida Avenue, on the east by Fourth Street, on the south by St. Mary's Road, and on the west by First Street; directly south of Memorial Stadium.

COST: $6,330,000.

FINANCED: Through the sale of revenue bonds, to be retired through student fees and income from the building, without benefit of state tax funds.

OPENING: With an Open House, 1:30 to 5 p.m. and 7:30 to 11 p.m. Saturday, March 2, 1963; Illinois-Iowa basketball game, 8 p. m. Monday, March 4; and Illinois-Iowa basketball game Saturday, March 9.

DEDICATION: Honors DAY, Friday, May 3, 1963.

CAPACITY: About 17,675, including 1,500 portable plastic chairs on activity floor; 15,910 permanent seats; plus 147 for spectators in wheelchairs; 76 representatives of press and radio; for a total of 16,725 fixed seating. For University of Illinois Commencement, including the platform, seating will be 17,500. There is a theater quadrant of 4,142.

EXHIBITION S P A C E: 60,000 square feet on the concourse.

ENTRANCES: T h r e e dual ramps on the north, east and south sides; with a single ramp on the west side, plus lower level entrance; canopy is to the west side.

curtains to be lowered from the overhead grid, there may be stage shows, concerts, recitals, ballets, and many other cultural events from a stage. Commencement, convocations, large meetings, and other gatherings are planned for the structure.

Getting their first view of the interior of the Assembly Hall, visitors also will have an opportunity on Saturday, if they wish, to sit down in the auditorium and listen to the entertainment — either just portions of it, or the entire program.

Visitors will be free to roam the building, hear about its construction, and see the unusual features of the world-wonder. There will be announcements by Henry Lippold, WILL-TV news director. Assisting the planning committee in preparation and presentation of the program is Bill Dale, TV producer for WILL-TV.

Announcing the performances will be Stanton Saltzman, producer - director of the Office of Instructional Television.

The program includes:

1:45 p.m. — Drill by Pershing Rifles.

2 p.m. — Presentation by the UI Concert Band under the direction of Prof. Mark H. Hindsley.

7:45 p.m. — Demonstration by the Illinois Fencing Team directed by Coach Max Garret.

2:15 p.m. — Performance by the Men's Glee Club under the direction of Harold Woodward.

8:45 p.m. — Performance by the Women's Glee Club under the direction of Ralph Woodward.

3:15 p.m. — Demonstration of trampoline and tumbling by Illini Gymnastics Team under the direction of Charlie Pond.

4:15 p.m. — Performance by the Jazz Band directed by John Garvey.

In the evening visitors will have an opportunity to see the new Hall and to hear a program by professional talent, augmented by student participants.

J. J. Johnson and the Jazz Band and Les Paul and Mary Ford, recording artists, will entertain between 7:30 and 11 p.m.

The Open House will be characterized by informality. No tickets will be required.

Dean Theodore B. Peterson of the University of Illinois College of Journalism and Communications is chairman of the

(Please turn to Page 5, Col. 1)

INTERIOR VIEW OF GIANT ASSEMBLY HALL
. . . 12 stories high from floor to dome above grid and catwalks

Builder's 'Most Memorable Job'

By ROGER EBERT
News-Gazette Staff Writer

The builders at Felmley-Dickerson Construction Co. may tackle many vast projects in the years to come—but none will have quite the romance of the new University of Illinois Assembly Hall.

"It was the most memorable project we've ever taken on," says president Ray Dickerson, who helped found the firm in 1935.

"It was a constant challenge, and it will be unforgettable for those who worked on it."

Dickerson's firm then considered dozens of alternate plans f o r building the great structure designed by architect Max Abramovitz, which includes the largest unsupported dome in the world.

Engineers, sketching various step-by-step methods, discarded the traditional dome construction method of building the dome over a mound of earth and then removing the earth.

Instead, they finally decided on a line of approach that included these basic steps:

1. Digging out the area for the ring footing.

2. Pouring the ring footing, and then setting the giant concrete buttresses.

3. Constructing the concrete corrugation for the stadium seating level, down to a point 25 feet above the eventual playing floor.

4. In the meantime, pouring concrete walls, slabs and floors as became necessary in the progress of the construction.

5. Then, pouring the great dome, section by section.

6. After completion of the dome, removing the rest of the earth inside the structure by assembling a crane inside.

7. Finishing the seats down to the playing level, and then putting the final inside touches on the building.

The first spade of earth for the Assembly Hall was turned in June 1959. Repeated strikes, at both a national and local level, delayed completion until spring of 1963.

Dickerson said the strong interior tower, used to support the dome until the rim of the building was wrapped with wire, was the "most unusual feature" of the construction process.

"Instead, I would say our biggest inspiration was leaving 24 feet of dirt inside the building until the dome was completed," he said.

"By this means, we kept the inside f l o o r at ground level making it much easier to travel in and out. We avoided the problem of rains, because i t h r e excavation had been dug first we would have had a lake inside for months. And we gained the psychological advantage of working over dirt instead of concrete."

Dickerson said the remaining dirt floor also made for a gain in the amount of frustration and the work went along," he said.

"We ourselves had a certain mix, Felmley-Dickerson is responsible for the Illini Union addition, the Electrical Engineering building, the new Chemistry Annex, the Veterinary Medicine building, Sevier Hall dome economics building), the C h i l d Development laboratory, Allen Residence Hall, the Men's Residence Halls and food services building north of Memorial Stadium, the seven - story high-rise graduate residence hall on Green St., the student - staff apartments on Green, and the Education Building, still in progress.

Locally, the company has built Holy Cross School, Birch V i l lage, the McKinley-B r a d l e y housing development and the Moose Hall, among others.

It constructed the rocket area at Chanute AFB in 1954-55.

And at the University of Illi-

(Please turn to Page 5, Col. 8)

4
The Assembly Hall
Opens for Business

Open house

The initial public viewing of the Assembly Hall was primarily a time for sightseeing. On March 2, 1963, the building was opened for the first time to the public at no charge from 1:30-5:00 p.m. and again from 7:30-11:00 p.m. A total of 39,317 persons went through the turnstiles during the two sessions. Their ages ranged from 4 weeks to 88 years old.

There was no formal entertainment program for the open house, although the UI Concert Band, the UI Jazz Band and the glee clubs performed, as did trombonist J. J. Johnson and recording artists Les Paul and Mary Ford, a husband-wife team who subsequently received a star on the Hollywood Walk of Fame.

The public debut occurred on a milestone day for the UI, which was opened (as Illinois Industrial University) 95 years earlier on March 2, 1868, with 50 students and three faculty members. By 1963, the student enrollment had increased to more than 24,000. The $20 per-semester fee charged to students for the hall raised roughly $1 million annually. About half of that total went toward the cost of the building, with the remainder funneled to general operating expenses.

Photo courtesy of the Champaign County Historical Archives, The Urbana Free Library, Urbana, Illinois.

Photo courtesy of the Assembly Hall.

First events at the hall

Two 1963 Illini men's basketball games were played the following week at the Assembly Hall. Ticket manager George Legg had 135 ushers and 64 gatemen in place at the first home UI basketball game at the Assembly Hall. Each total was approximately twice the number used when the games were played at Huff Gym. There was no lack of interest in the positions. A newspaper ad, which first appeared in late February 1963, produced nearly 500 applicants.

Later in the year, the first of 33 IHSA boys' basketball state tournaments was hosted in the building. The opening prep tournament, a two-day, four-session extravaganza, attracted 64,255 spectators, with 16,183 on hand when Chicago Carver edged Centralia 53-52 to win the state championship.

Because there was no kitchen in the Assembly Hall, concessions such as hot dogs were made off-site and transported to the Hall for sale. "That spring, when we had the boys' basketball state tournament, we arranged with Central Foods to fix hot dogs at 5 or 6 o'clock in the morning," says Wayne Hecht, then an assistant director at the Assembly Hall. "We kept them in hot boxes, with sterno. We were still serving those at 6 o'clock at night. We're lucky we didn't kill someone." The food, incidentally, had to be consumed in the hallways. "You couldn't take them inside," Hecht recalls.

The first major non-sporting event was the Ice Capades (then in its 22nd year), which started a five-day run on April 16, 1963.

Dedication

The university waited until May 3, 1963, to hold its official dedication ceremony. The featured speaker was Pulitzer Prize-winning poet Carl Sandburg, 85, who received three standing ovations from the estimated crowd of 8,000.

Shortly after the three-month anniversary of its opening, the Class of 1963 (2,850 strong) became the first group to hold its commencement ceremony inside the Assembly Hall on June 15, 1963. Attendance was estimated at 13,000.

Photo courtesy of the Assembly Hall.

Photo courtesy of the Assembly Hall.

Photo courtesy of the Assembly Hall.

Attendance records

Officials predicted that the Assembly Hall would be well-received by people with different interests. That belief was illustrated by the attendance figures for the 1964-65 school year. The turnout for sporting events was 164,624. The number of spectators at entertainment events was 145,724 and the total for conventions, meetings and conferences was 135,786.

During the 1966-67 school year, the range was 201,874 for entertainment events, 142,810 for sporting events and 112,672 for conferences and conventions.

5
Updates and Improvements

Changes to the roof

The greatest source of consternation once the Assembly Hall was opened was the roof. It has required regular maintenance. A rubber, waterproof coating of neoprene was applied, followed by spraying hypalon, a synthetic rubber designed to increase resistance to water. The coating was applied with high-pressure paint sprayers with an eye to the weather. If conditions are too hot, the hypalon will bubble, but if temperatures are too cold, it will not adhere properly.

In May 1964, 14 months after the grand opening, black spots and water bubbles were detected on the roof. It was still under a five-year warranty from the Corrosion Control Co. of New York, but the business had gone bankrupt so UI officials had to look elsewhere.

Bids were taken for re-roofing because the original surface was not water tight. Bubbling and discoloration were among the problems observed.

The lowest bid of $133,107 was the one accepted. The Phillips Roofing Co. from Oklahoma City, which previously had roofed the Houston Astrodome, finished their work in 1967. However, from 1968-74, the company returned to town each summer for repair work.

In 1975, a report indicated bubbles had formed between the undercoat and the upper coat. If not attended to, water seepage would ultimately become a problem. Estimates to recoat the entire roof, including the ridges, were set at $300,000. In 1979, bids were solicited again, with UI allocating $1.6 million for this project and other improvements.

This time, rather than spraying on the materials, the plan was to apply sheets of hypalon and neoprene. The work, combined with adding some new seats, permanent concession stands, and new 80-foot curtains to be used for stage productions, was finished in 1981. The curtains cost $87,000. The 4,000 new seats, in the west-side theater quadrant, came with a $397,000 price tag. The old

Photo courtesy of the Assembly Hall.

Robert Sarver, UI roofer from Facilities and Services, scrapes the roof of the Assembly Hall on July 19, 2011. Photo courtesy *The News-Gazette*/Vanda Bidwell.

seats were not discarded, but rotated into various parts of the B section.

By contrast, when seats were originally purchased, $253,000 was paid to the American Seating Co. of New York, for 17,000 seats.

Parking fees

On the first-year anniversary of the Assembly Hall opening, *The News-Gazette* reported in its March 2, 1964, editions that two of the four parking lots were scheduled to enact toll parking later in the spring. The fee was 10 cents for 24 hours. The two lots where the automatic gate meters were not installed were closed off during the day.

In the early 1990s, parking fees became a controversial topic when the four lots surrounding the building underwent a $2 million renovation project. The repaving work and improved lighting were completed in 1992.

At that time, there was a charge for parking in the lots during the day ($1.25 per day or $160 for a yearly pass), but not for evening games or performances. A $3 per-vehicle charge was the proposal for events. Assembly Hall director Wayne Hecht estimated the charge could generate about $300,000 per year.

Estimates in 2013 are that parking generates approximately $325,000 annually.

Air conditioning

Another long-standing issue is the lack of air conditioning in the Assembly Hall. Currently only office spaces are air conditioned. Air conditioning wasn't included in the original plans, and the lack of a cooling system cost the UI opportunities to host summer events when the East Central Illinois air temperatures can be unbearable. During the 1988-89 school year, five conventions declined to meet in Champaign-Urbana because the Assembly Hall was not air conditioned. In a September 19, 1989, *News-Gazette* article, Marie Earley, director of the convention and visitors bureau, estimated that those decisions could have meant "$10 million to $13 million lost in local business."

In 1990, officials estimated that to air condition the entire building would cost between $3 and 5 million. The talk ended soon thereafter. Air conditioning is, however, among the items considered in renovating the Hall.

Scoreboards and court floor

The original scoreboard installed at the Assembly Hall was used through the 1990-91 season. It was replaced by a $450,000 scoreboard that was donated to the university (by White Way Sign Co., from Chicago) in exchange for 10-year rights to the eight scoreboard advertising panels.

Prior to the 2004-05 basketball season, a new video board and matrix were installed at a cost of $1.7 million.

The original basketball court was used until late in the 1986-87 season. A new $75,000 maple court was unveiled for the February 5, 1987, game against Northwestern. The floor consists of 232 individual panels (4-by-8 feet, each weighing 100 pounds) that are pieced together. New baskets and backstops made an appearance that night as well.

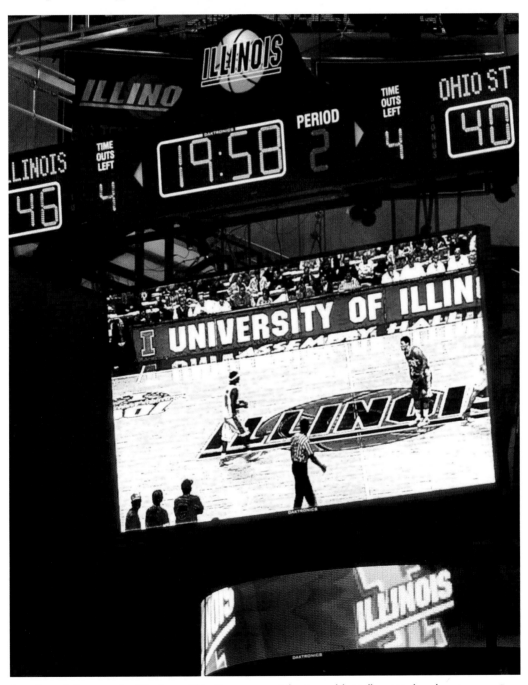

Scoreboard shown at the Illinois vs. Ohio State game at the Assembly Hall on Wednesday, January 5, 2005. Photo courtesy of *The News-Gazette*/Robin Scholz.

Outdoor signage

The outdoor Assembly Hall sign on the northwest corner of the property, which promotes upcoming events, was erected in November 1989. Interestingly, the sign was briefly shown in the 1992 music video for Metallica's popular song, "Wherever I May Roam."

Larry Fossel of Sign Productions guides the new sign down at the Assembly Hall. It was built by Daktronics from Brookings, South Dakota, and delivered and installed by Sign Productions from Cedar Rapids. February 10, 2006. Photo courtesy of *The News-Gazette*/Vanda Bidwell.

PART TWO

THE ASSEMBLY HALL BECOMES AN ENTERTAINMENT HUB

Robert Goulet played at the Assembly Hall on November 13, 1965. Victor Borge appeared six times, Peter Nero three times and the Mantovani Orchestra twice. Photo courtesy of the Assembly Hall.

6
Memorable Music and Stage Moments

Elvis Presley was called the King for good reason.

His 1976 show at the Assembly Hall remains the biggest in the arena's 50-year history, holding the one-night attendance record. It drew a standing-room crowd of more than 17,000 fans. One wrote that the "crowd was as much to see as Elvis."

"The top show was Elvis and that will not be duplicated," Assembly Hall director Kevin Ullestad said while listing the largest events in the arena's history.

Presley would die the year after his Assembly Hall concert. At the Hall he "wowed the enthusiastic audience with a mixture of songs ranging from some of his best-known old hits to more recent selections, including his latest release, 'Hurt,'" *News-Gazette* photographer Joe Wilske wrote in the caption of his photo of the King in a white jumpsuit.

Besides Elvis, nearly every other big name in entertainment (except the Beatles) has graced the Assembly Hall stage. Apparently they did not believe famed psychic Jeane Dixon's prediction that the newly built Assembly Hall, because of its radical concrete dome design, would collapse.

Mega-acts that have come to the Hall include Bruce "The Boss" Springsteen, Cher, the Rolling Stones, the Grateful Dead, Elton John, Bob Dylan (three times), the Moody Blues, the Beach Boys, Jethro Tull, Johnny Cash (six times), New Kids on the Block, Eminem, Jay-Z, Ludacris, REO Speedwagon, Dan Fogelberg and U2.

Among country acts that have entertained there are Dolly Parton, Alan Jackson (eight times), Kenny Chesney, Kenny Rogers, Garth Brooks, Shania Twain, and Reba McEntire, who one fan remembers was driven onto the stage in a real taxi cab. The country and now Broadway star performed here three times, twice in the 90s and once in 2000.

And let's not forget the iconic Frank Sinatra, who performed at the Hall in 1990, in the twilight of his sensational career, as part of a brief tour that included only three Midwest stops. A 35-piece orchestra accompanied "The Voice," then 75. Tickets for the first six rows were $100 each, at the time an unheard of amount, according to former Hall director Xen Riggs.

The Assembly Hall presents 25 to 30 national acts during each academic year. That includes popular musicians and comedians and also really big shows such as Monster Truck nationals and the Hot Rod Thunder Nationals; the Ice Capades — 21 times in the Hall's early years; Ringling Brothers/Barnum & Bailey Circus, which has brought its big ring into the Hall at least 21 times too; and the famous theatrical circus troupe Cirque du Soleil, which performed here in 2007, 2010 and 2012. Who has to go to Las Vegas to see Soleil?

Other national acts that have come to the Assembly Hall, some numerous times, are touring Broadway shows such as "Les Miserables," "Cats" and "The Producers"; Lord of the Dance, a celebration of Irish dance and music; and the Lipizzaner Stallions, who have galloped into the arena at least 10 times.

Cher performs at Assembly Hall on Tuesday, February 15, 2000. Photo courtesy of the Assembly Hall/Travis Bullock.

New Kids on the Block performed twice at the Assembly Hall. First on November 8, 1990, then again on July 5, 2009. Photo courtesy of the Assembly Hall/Ramzi Dreessen.

Hip hop artist Jay-Z performs at Assembly Hall on November 12, 2009. Photo courtesy of the Assembly Hall/Brad Meyer.

Ludacris performed March 1, 2004, and September 22, 2006. Photo courtesy of the Assembly Hall.

Les Paul and Mary Ford at the 1963 Assembly Hall Open House. Photo courtesy of the Assembly Hall.

ABOVE AND LEFT: Lawrence Welk entertained the crowd at Assembly Hall three different times in the past 50 years. These photos are believed to have been taken at the June 1, 1975, performance. Welk also performed June 11, 1978 and June 11, 1982. Photos courtesy of the Assembly Hall.

Prince performed at the Assembly Hall only once, April 10, 2004. Photo courtesy of the Assembly Hall.

Melissa Etheridge in concert on November 16, 1990. She did a second performance on May 1, 1994. Photo courtesy of the Assembly Hall.

Journey performed on May 1, 1980, October 2, 1981, October 5, 1986 and December 4, 2005. Photo courtesy of the Assembly Hall.

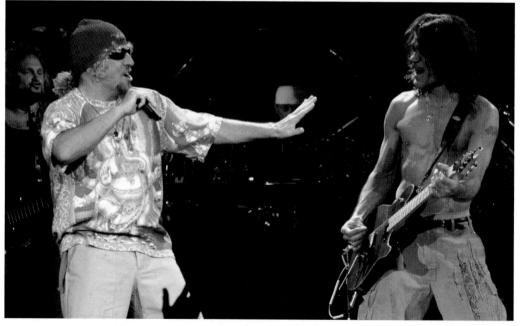

Singer Sammy Hagar (left) and guitarist Eddie Van Halen of the rock group Van Halen perform for the Assembly Hall crowd on September 21, 2004. The group played many of their classic hits. Photo courtesy of the Assembly Hall/Mike Salwan.

Karen Carpenter, 1975. Photo courtesy of the Assembly Hall.

Garth Brooks with an Illini basketball jersey he received at the press conference the night before his concert, March 7, 1997. Photo courtesy of *The News-Gazette*/Robert K. O'Daniell.

Alan Jackson in concert at the Assembly Hall on November 20, 2003. Photo courtesy of the Assembly Hall/Elizabeth Power.

Country artist Martina McBride performs at the Assembly Hall on February 22, 2008. Photo courtesy of the Assembly Hall/Josh Birnbaum.

Kenny Rogers has performed at the Assembly Hall 10 times, beginning in 1972. Photo courtesy of the Assembly Hall.

Country star Kenny Chesney performed each year from 2002-2005. Photo courtesy of the Assembly Hall.

Barry Manilow singing with a fan on stage at the Assembly Hall. Photo courtesy of the Assembly Hall.

Joan Jett performed at the Assembly Hall while co-headlining with Cheap Trick on March 28, 2008. Photo courtesy of the Assembly Hall/ Johnny Chiang.

Bob Hope, shown in November 1969 while in Champaign to give a performance at the Assembly Hall on November 8, 1969. Photo courtesy of the Assembly Hall.

In honor of Dad's weekend, Bill Cosby performed in front of a large crowd at the Assembly Hall on November 8, 2004. Before the show, Cosby was given a t-shirt and other items from the Illini track and field team and was made an honorary track member. Cosby's response, "As long as I don't have to do the workout!" Photo courtesy of The Assembly Hall/Mike Salwan.

Comedian ventriloquist Jeff Dunham and his puppet Walter perform on stage at the Assembly Hall on March 4, 2010. Photo courtesy of the Assembly Hall/Brad Meyer.

Comedian Lewis Black performed at the Assembly Hall on Friday, October 6, 2011. Photo courtesy of the Assembly Hall/Joshua Beckman.

The Ringling
Brothers/
Barnum &
Bailey Circus
has come to
the Assembly
Hall 17 times
beginning in
September of
1968. Photo
courtesy of the
Assembly Hall.

Tom Parkinson, the first Assembly Hall
director, was a circus fan. Photo courtesy of the Assembly Hall.

Photo courtesy of the Assembly Hall.

The third largest entertainment arena in Illinois, and the biggest one downstate, can accommodate the huge acts, thanks to first Hall director Tom Parkinson, a circus fan who insisted to architect
Max Abramovitz that a tunnel, rather than elevator, would be a better way to move equipment. That
was solidified further when the Assembly Hall renovated its one-truck loading dock to a three-truck
dock, Ullestad said. That would allow giant acts with a lot of equipment to load in and out quickly
so as to be on their way to their next venue.

Because of the expanded loading dock, the Hall was able to present the rock band Aerosmith in
1998 and 2001, and Janet Jackson in 2002. Those were the two biggest rock acts to hit the Assembly
Hall, with 14 semi-trucks of equipment each.

The Assembly Hall had to build a tunnel of another sort for popular singer Barry Manilow. It led
from his dressing room to the stage. Manilow, who entertained five times at the Hall between 1980
and 2000, didn't want crew members or anyone else looking at him as he walked to the stage.

Other "riders" in contracts negotiated by the Assembly Hall and stars' managers included some
interesting requests:

One of the Ice Capades performers backstage in 1965. The Ice Capades have been to the Assembly Hall 30 times in the past 50 years. Photo courtesy of the Assembly Hall.

Lord of the Dance performer. Photo courtesy of the Assembly Hall.

ABOVE: Monster Trucks in the Assembly Hall. Photo courtesy of the Assembly Hall.

LEFT: Some of the cast of Les Miserables. Photo courtesy of the Assembly Hall.

- Neil Young asked for a washer and dryer.
- Elvis Presley's demands were modest: a six-pack of Coca-Cola.
- Journey wanted dinner served an hour before show time and ordered shrimp and cauliflower au gratin.
- Lawrence Welk asked for a bed in his dressing room so he could take a nap before going on stage.
- And perhaps most famously, Van Halen, who performed at the Hall in 1980 and 2004, asked for a 3-pound bag of M&Ms, with all the brown ones removed.

Comedian Bob Newhart specified the type of microphone he wanted to use. He was among many famous comedians who entertained at the Assembly Hall. One of the first was Allan Sherman, a folk singer/comedian who had studied journalism at the UI and was famous for his "Hello Muddah, Hello Faddah" song. He revised that with Illini lyrics for his 1963 show at the Hall, which was reviewed by Roger Ebert, then a UI student and *News-Gazette* staff writer. "He brought down the house

The Assembly Hall loading dock expanded from a one-truck dock to a three-truck dock, which allowed it to attract even larger entertainment acts. Photo courtesy of *The News-Gazette*/Darrell Hoemann.

Billy Graham and the Intervarsity Christian Fellowship at the Assembly Hall. Photo courtesy of the Assembly Hall/Ellen Steele.

The 1965 University of Illinois Commencement. Photo courtesy of the Assembly Hall.

time and time again and turned his personal homecoming into an opportunity for Illinis — new and old — to count their traditions," Ebert wrote.

The now famous movie critic reported that a 22-piece orchestra provided "comical orchestration" for Sherman's parodies of well-known songs, and that the New Christy Minstrels, a folk ensemble, also performed. But the show belonged to Allan Sherman, Ebert reported. After it was over, Sherman said he had never been so nervous in his life. He also said the Assembly Hall was "one of those buildings that come along once in lifetime."

During his lifetime, famed comedian Bob Hope performed five times at the Hall between 1965 and 1990. He was 87 when he made his last appearance there and "brought the crowd back to a never-never time familiar to his television viewers in which Jerry Ford is the bumbling, kindly president, Zsa-Zsa Gabor the reigning sex queen and Phyllis Diller an up-and-coming young comic. Only Boy George served to remind us of the 80s, and Saddam Hussein filled in as comic villain," *News-Gazette* reporter Paul Wood wrote in his review.

Jerry Lewis was there in 1993. Red Skelton came in 1985, shopping beforehand at local stores to buy props for his show. Steve Martin came in 1977, and many people in the audience came wearing arrows through their heads, false noses and glasses and carried balloons in their hands — all nods to Martin's routine.

George Carlin brought his irreverent act to the Assembly Hall twice in the 70s and once in the early 90s. Bill Cosby brought his clean but funny act to the Hall five times between 1968 and 2004.

Among younger generations of comedians to tickle funny bones at the Assembly Hall were Eddie Murphy, in 1985 and 1987; Carlos Mencia in 2006; and Adam Sandler for a free student show in 1994. Seth Meyers, co-head writer for TV's *Saturday Night Live*, appeared during the fall semester 2012.

The Assembly Hall hasn't presented just mid-brow entertainment. Three-time Pulitzer Prize-winning poet Carl Sandburg helped open the new building on May 31, 1963. Among other high-brow acts were ballet companies, including the American Ballet Theater, which performed six times at the Hall in the 60s and early 70s. Famous ballet dancer Mikhail Baryshnikov brought his White Oak Dance Project to the Hall in 1991. Rudolf Nureyev preceded him, dancing at the Hall in 1973 in a National Ballet of Canada production of "Sleeping Beauty."

Among world-class orchestras that performed at the Hall during its earlier years were the New

York Philharmonic led by Leonard Bernstein, in 1967, and the Chicago Symphony Orchestra. It performed there six times.

In the 1960s the Assembly Hall also presented avant-garde happenings. Composer John Cage, in-residence at the UI School of Music, staged a four-and-a-half-hour happening in 1967 with the Merce Cunningham Dance Company, one of the most influential modern-dance companies of the 20th century. Both showed off their "chance" music and dance compositions. In 1969, Cage also presented his famous piece "HPSCHD" at the Hall. *The News-Gazette* billed it as a "marathon optic and aural extravaganza." It included "multimedia environment multiple screenings of art films and visual design" by no less than Andy Warhol.

And even LSD advocate/free-love guru Timothy Leary entertained at the saucer-shaped building, in 1968. "Love's where it's at," he told the 4,974 people who showed up. "We've lost the love thread in the great mechanical freak out. If you don't learn how to move in the replaceable parts generation, they will move you."

He urged students, though, to refrain from using LSD until he could turn on Lyndon Baines Johnson at the 1968 Democratic National Convention, to happen that summer in Chicago. Now that's history.

The Assembly Hall has been home to more serious events as well. In 1990, Robert Redford came not as an actor but as an environmentalist, to speak at Catalyst, the student environmental conference. Also speaking at that event were Ralph Nader, the Rev. Jesse Jackson and Helen Caldicott. Redford drew a standing ovation from the 7,000 students in attendance. He told them he no longer trusted the word "progress."

"At a certain point we have to ask ourselves whether we've been the beneficiaries of progress or the victims," he said. "We've messed up the air, the land and the water in our passion to control things." He went on to say "I'm not a prophet of gloom and doom. But I've always assumed a love of land and a love of country go together."

Altogether the Assembly Hall does 100 events a year, including the big-name acts, basketball games and student shows such as the Central Black Student Union's Cotton Club revue, the Illini Union Board spring musicals and the Marching Illini in Concert.

It's also a venue for community events. Retired banker Ed Scharlau gives his "state of the local economy" talk during the annual Busey Bank Seminar at the Assembly Hall. There are business expo and home shows, and when Christmas rolls around every year you can expect the Chris Cringle Craft Fair.

Campus Crusade for Christ and the Intervarsity Christian Fellowship have had large conventions at the Hall, with the Rev. Billy Graham speaking at five of the Intervarsity conferences between 1967 and 1990.

The Junior Academy of Science has met annually at the Hall, too, since it opened. And UI students both start and end their academic careers at the Assembly Hall, where the UI New Student Convocation takes place each fall and the UI Commencement, takes place each spring.

Champaign Centennial and Central and Urbana high schools have their graduation ceremonies there each spring, too. "My best memory is graduating from Urbana High School in the Assembly Hall," one former student wrote. "It was so big that anyone in your family can come in and watch, and every seat at the Assembly Hall is a good seat."

By Melissa Merli with Fred Kroner

7
The Community Welcomes President Clinton to the Hall

Just two days after news broke in early 1998 about the Monica Lewinsky scandal, President Bill Clinton came to the University of Illinois. He spoke at the Assembly Hall, the only place big enough for all the folks who wanted to see him. Students, community members and even people from out of town packed the place, having picked up more than 12,000 free tickets.

Another 8,000 people went to the nearby Intramural Physical Education building, better known as IMPE, to watch Clinton on closed-circuit TV. Still hundreds, maybe thousands of others who waited in line in the cold were unable to get into either venue, resulting in disappointed ticket holders.

Those who turned out to see Clinton and Vice President Al Gore gave them what they sorely needed: a warm Midwest welcome. Many reporters described the presidential visit as a pep rally or love fest. Even the hundreds of people who lined the motorcade route from Willard Airport to the Assembly Hall gave the president and his entourage a hero's welcome.

U.S. Senator Dick Durbin (a democrat from Illinois), who was in the procession, saw only one negative sign along the route. "Having been through a lot of these motorcades, that was phenomenal," he told reporters.

Also here for the speech was CBS reporter and Illinois native Harry Smith, who noted that the media attention was "unquestioningly" bigger for the president's visit because of the Lewinsky controversy. Smith later told *The News-Gazette* he "was struck by the fact there were no boos, no catcalls." He said, "Bill Clinton's almost like a rock star."

Like others who got free tickets to hear the president, David Brenner, then a UI computer science major, said Clinton's sex life was a distraction from what was most important to him and other folks. "I'm much more interested in what he has to say about education and the economy," Brenner said.

People also were just psyched to see a sitting president, a once-in-a-lifetime opportunity for most. Clinton's visit marked only the third time that a president in power came to Champaign-Urbana. William Howard Taft was here in 1911; he met with the UI president. Gerald Ford came in 1976, just 13 years after the Assembly Hall went up, bypassing it and the university to speak at Champaign Centennial High School.

Clinton was the first and so far only president to speak at the Assembly Hall while in office, though other politicians, as well as Clinton's wife, Hillary Rodham Clinton,

Photo courtesy of *The News-Gazette.*

Photo courtesy of *The News-Gazette.*

Sam Donaldson talking to various spectators.
Photo courtesy of *The News-Gazette*.

Fans cheer for the president and vice president at the Assembly Hall.
Photo courtesy of *The News-Gazette*/Robin Scholz.

LEFT TO RIGHT: President Bill Clinton, Senator Carol Mosley Braun, Vice President Al Gore, and Senator Dick Durbin at the door of Air Force One. Photo courtesy of *The News-Gazette*.

have taken the podium there. Three years before her husband would visit, First Lady Hillary Rodham Clinton spoke at the UI commencement.

Among other politicians to have stumped or spoken at the Assembly Hall since it opened in 1963 were Illinois governors Otto Kerner and Richard Ogilvie; U.S. Senator Paul Simon, a beloved Illinois democrat; and Adlai Stevenson II, at the time the U.S. ambassador to the United Nations.

In an interesting political side note, actor Dustin Hoffman spoke at the Hall in April 1968 on behalf of the Eugene McCarthy presidential campaign. At the time, Hoffman was one of the best-known actors on the planet, having been nominated for an Academy Award the year before as best actor in *The Graduate*.

UI officials weren't told why Clinton chose to speak at Illinois. Some said the leader of the free

A capacity crowd listens to President Bill Clinton's speech on January 28, 1998, at the Assembly Hall. Photo courtesy of *The News-Gazette*/John Dixon.

world might have picked the university to underscore the education themes in his State of the Union address, which he delivered the night before he came to Champaign. Or, that Clinton chose to speak on the UI campus because Al Gore had appeared there the year before for a televised town meeting with students to push the administration's financial aid programs.

An advance team from the White House came a week ahead of time to scope out the campus and the Assembly Hall. The Secret Service "swept" the giant building, looking for potential dangers. Assembly Hall staff did everything they were ordered to do. The university added up to 100 phone lines to the Hall to accommodate the White House, television networks and national media. Up to a dozen more lines were added outside for satellite trucks.

The UI public affairs office handed out media credentials to more than 300 media members, ranging from the Urbana High School student newspaper, *The Echo*, to the Tokyo Broadcasting System. Among big-media stars who picked up a pass was ABC TV's Sam Donaldson, who entertained reporters by cracking jokes in the press room of the Assembly Hall. There, 30 aspiring journalists — UI students — worked as volunteers. Another 200 volunteers from student government and the College Democrats helped with ushering and crowd control inside the Hall.

Vice President Al Gore salutes the crowd during his speech at the Assembly Hall. Photo courtesy of *The News-Gazette*/Robin Scholz.

Police from Urbana, Champaign, Champaign County, the UI and outlying towns provided security. "It's an enormous detail. No one agency could really do this by themselves," said then UI Police Chief Krystal Fitzpatrick. "Having the president here is the top level of security." The only thing bigger, she said, was the first Farm Aid concert in 1985 at Memorial Stadium, only because of the sheer number of people — 80,000 — who turned out to hear mega-stars such as Willie Nelson, John Mellencamp and Bob Dylan.

As they most likely did at Farm Aid, Clinton and Vice President Al Gore felt the love upon arriving at Willard Airport and then the Assembly Hall. At Willard, among those greeting the president and VP were a dozen "local heroes" selected for recognition by the White House. They included:

President Clinton listens to Carol Mosley Braun on stage during Vice President Al Gore's speech. Photo courtesy of *The News-Gazette*/Robin Scholz.

President Clinton shakes hands with Rev. Steve Shoemaker. Photo courtesy of *The News-Gazette*.

President Clinton and Vice President Al Gore listening to speakers prior to their time to address the crowd. Photo courtesy of *The News-Gazette*.

Tim Boeker of Champaign and Stacy Turaniak of Urbana cheer as President Clinton stands to speak at the Assembly Hall. Photo courtesy of *The News-Gazette*.

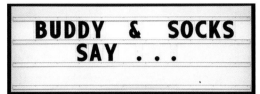

Mark Fisher, then owner of Animal Outfitters, puts the last letters in place on the business' sign along Rt. 45 in Savoy with a message to President Clinton. Photo courtesy of *The News-Gazette*/John Dixon.

- Willie Summerville and his wife, Val, for their work with youths in the black community.
- Carle's Dr. Curtis Krock, honored for his care of patients, including making house calls.
- Ann Bishop, co-founder of Prairienet, recognized for her efforts to involve low-income families and children in using computers and shaping computer technology. She gave Clinton a Prairienet account.
- The Rev. Steve Shoemaker, for his work with the homeless.

The honorees rode in the presidential motorcade. Police lined the route and blocked off U.S. 45 at the airport. But early birds were able to drive in and park outside the main terminal to watch the presidential planes arrive.

"We just want to see the president," said Joe Pelszynski of Danville. "We've never seen the president before. We just hope to catch sight of the plane so we can tell people back home."

Once Clinton, Gore and other dignitaries arrived at the Assembly Hall, they saw orange and blue banners that read "Illinois Welcomes President Clinton" and "Illinois Welcomes Back Vice President Gore." A larger, red, white and blue banner on stage proclaimed, "Preparing America for the 21st Century."

Once Clinton and Gore entered the Hall, people chanted "Bill, Bill, Bill" and "We love you, Bill." Even Gore must have felt uplifted. He was said to lose his stiff demeanor while he fired up the crowd before the president spoke.

"When he got really worked up," Clinton later said, "I thought I wished I had people walking in the aisles and passing plates." Clinton also praised the UI Pep Band. It played the national anthem and "Hail to the Chief" when he walked into the Hall. (In one of the odder moments building up to he speech, the Pep Band played, "Carry on My Wayward Son.")

Despite that, Clinton told the crowd, "I wish I could take the pep band with me the next month or two." As flash bulbs popped, Clinton asked the mostly student crowd to support several issues, among them education, technology research and Social Security reform.

"You represent what we're trying to build for the future of America," he told the audience. He and Gore also paid tribute to the UI and Champaign-Urbana as a major hub of technology development. Clinton mentioned Larry Smarr, then director of the National Center for Supercomputing Applications, for his and the center's role in developing the next generation of the Internet.

"Illinois and all the other land-grant colleges have literally led our way into the Information Age," Clinton said. More specifically, Clinton asked the Assembly Hall audience to support his efforts to:

- Make a college education as universal as a high school education.
- Increase funding for medical research through the National Science Foundation and the National Cancer Institute.
- Make elementary and secondary schools as highly regarded as American universities. He repeated his call for 100,000 new elementary school teachers to lower class sizes in first, second and third grades.
- Address the problem of global warming and climate change.
- Expand access to child care.

Regarding Social Security, Clinton admitted that when he was young he never thought much about retirement. But he told the students in the audience that the funding uncertainties of Social Security would affect them as much as anybody else. He repeated his call to use any budget surplus for Social Security funding.

Playing to the higher education crowd, Clinton recounted how he and Congress expanded the Pell grant program, provided 300,000 new work-study jobs, made interest on student loans tax-deductible, and created tax cuts to help families pay for college expenses.

After the speech, Clinton and Gore waved to people on all sides of the Assembly Hall, drawing cheers, whistles and applause. The ovation lasted several minutes; Clinton stood still for a few moments, seeming to bask in the warmth.

During his speech the president had made no mention of the Lewinsky controversy. But when Gore introduced Clinton, the vice president said, "I ask all of you to join me in supporting him and standing by his side."

The visit was Clinton's 15th to the state of Illinois. He said he was delighted to be back. "This state has been very good to me in many ways," he said. And of C-U and the UI, he said, "I don't know how in all my roaming across America I have never lit down here before, but I sure am glad I got here today."

Clinton later told the Associated Press that he had "an incredible day" in Champaign. But, it ended on a sluggish note: Before he could fly to his next stop in Wisconsin, Air Force One became stuck in the mud while taxiing for takeoff from Willard.

By Melissa Merli and The News-Gazette

An Air Force Crewman surveys the landing gear of Air Force One, which sank into soft mud on the taxi way at Willard Airport. Photo by Teak Phillips.

Air Force One, with President Clinton aboard, roars off the end of the runway at Willard Airport Wednesday afternoon, January 28, 1998. The plane is taking off over the former Air Force One which lies crippled on the taxiway, stuck in the mud when its right main landing gear ran off the pavement with the President aboard. Photo courtesy of *The News-Gazette*/John Dixon.

8
The Backstage Team Makes
It Happen at the Hall

Behind the scenes, there were — and still are — dozens of Assembly Hall employees who never made a basket or held the microphone while 17,000 spectators were screaming in unison. They were instrumental, however, in the games and shows taking place in a professional manner, with a sound system correctly adjusted and seeing that all other details, such as lights and power, were attended to with precise accuracy.

John Page, whose 20 years as a staffer included 10 as a full-time stage hand, says it's easy to tell the skill level of his former coworkers. "So many local stage hands went on to bigger and better things," Page says. One was Jay Lipschutz, who handled audio for Ricky Skaggs and now works as production manager for Kathy Mattea.

It's not a surprise, Page believes, that those from the UI were in demand. "We did rock 'n roll and we did Broadway productions," Page recalls. "The Assembly Hall was one of the most unique venues and they had the foresight to put in a rigging system. We were getting first-run Broadway shows. It was easy to route them to Champaign as they were going from Indianapolis to Des Moines or from St. Louis to Chicago."

The public face of the Assembly Hall was its first director, Decatur native Tom Parkinson, a former editor at *Billboard* magazine. He was one of two full-time employees before there was an

John Page, left, with mother Murnie. Photo courtesy of *The News-Gazette*.

Assembly Hall building. During the construction stage, he was hired, as was Mary Claire Smith, an executive secretary and office manager. Parkinson and Smith started in September 1961, 18 months before the facility was finished.

Parkinson was 66 when he retired in August 1987. Page credits him as instrumental in helping the Assembly Hall gain a foothold with big-time acts. "His clout helped solidify Champaign-Urbana as one of the premier locations [for entertainers]," Page says. "We respected him."

Parkinson was responsible for one of the few deviations that architect Max Abramovitz allowed from his original design. His plans called for a large elevator to be used to move equipment from one level to another. Parkinson, a circus fan, was insistent that a tunnel would be a better option because an elephant could not fit into an elevator. Abramovitz relented, and a tunnel was figured into the plans one year before the building opened.

From the outset, Parkinson — whose first office as Assembly Hall director was located in the Illini Union — was confident the facility would be a godsend for the community. In 1962, he told *News-Gazette* staff writer Bill Lyon, "The Assembly Hall will put Champaign-Urbana in the same class with such metropolitan centers as Los Angeles, Cleveland and Philadelphia in terms of facilities to attract large numbers of people. The Assembly Hall puts us in the class of Madison Square Garden." Parkinson envisioned so many events that "it's going to be a challenge for those connected with the Assembly Hall to keep up with the schedules."

There was one event held at the Hall he probably never envisioned. When Parkinson died in 1993, the memorial service was held at the building where he worked for a quarter of a century.

The reputation of the Assembly Hall personnel was a major factor in Chicago-based JAM Productions sending so many acts to Champaign. "The Assembly Hall has a very professional staff," said Jerry Mickelson, from JAM Productions, in a 1982 *News-Gazette* interview. "The unloading and the rigging and all the work gets done the way it should be. . . . There's not anybody who ever complains about being there. A lot of groups are afraid to play colleges where students are the productions stage hands. The student crews will disappear or won't know how to get the job done right. In Champaign, it's professionals who are doing the work. People at the Assembly Hall know how to tap the market. They really do a great job."

Page, along with colleagues Dave Aldridge and Bill Beebe, wore multiple hats. The performers — and their production staffs — would "look to us for insight on how to fit their show into our building," Page says. "We were the stewards of the building." The requests ranged from typical — such as help with the lights — to the eccentric.

Entertainers occasionally wanted to see the various nooks and crannies of the Assembly Hall. Howie Mandel saw it from a perspective of few others during his August 29, 1992, appearance. "We took him up on the [overhanging] grid," Page says, "and he wanted to go out on the roof, so we let him take a look."

A huge electronic theater grid is suspended from the dome roof 85 feet above the floor. The structure is 50-by-94 feet. The catwalk surrounding the grid holds equipment for lighting.

The rock group Journey asked to see sites on the town. Page piled five members into his '55 Chevy and headed to Campustown. Group members scattered in different directions.

When it was time to meet up and return to the Assembly Hall for a late-afternoon sound check, drummer Steve Smith had not rejoined his band mates.

"Someone asked where the closest arcade was," Page says, "and we went there [Space Port Arcade, on Green St.] and found him. He was killing the machine and had something like 25 free games. Here was this famous drummer and six kids 11 to 15 were checking out his prowess on the Astroid machine."

Page enjoyed the various facets of his duties at the Assembly Hall, including the times he was hired as a runner. "The job of the runner was to find the unique requests," Page says. "The promoter might say, 'I need a box of yellow tooth picks, scented mint.'"

The most bizarre request during Page's watch came when rocker Ozzy Osbourne was in town on January 27, 1982. "I had to go to a local meat shop and get chopped liver and other raw meat they were going to throw in the first three rows," he says. That night, however, Osbourne collapsed on stage before his first song and was taken to Carle Foundation Hospital for observation. The show, which had a paid attendance of 3,115, was canceled and patrons were refunded their money. Osbourne was released later the same evening.

One frustration, Page remembers, was when Assembly Hall staff was asked their advice, but then the entertainers chose to ignore it. When Page was the facility's head rigger, he spoke with Jon Bon

Wes Thuney, an Urbana firefighter and past president of the Stagehands Union, pretending to fish on the ice in Assembly after an Ice Capades performance. Photo courtesy of the Assembly Hall/Doug Pugh.

Jovi in advance of his appearance. "Typically," Page says, "we'd do a north-end setup, but he wanted the stage facing west. We tried to talk him out of it." Bon Jovi was firm in his resolve, and got his wish. Afterward, Page says, "he complained about the set-up."

Page and his cohorts took a serious approach to their jobs, but when the work day was over, they weren't immune from having fun. "Doug Pugh and I loved to play practical jokes," Page says. When the Ice Capades ended one of their 1990s runs, Page and Pugh cut a hole in the ice, placed a fish nearby and staged Wes Thuney, an Urbana firefighter and past President of the Stagehands Union, sitting on a bucket next to it with a fishing pole.

It wasn't just Page's talented co-workers who were in demand. When Xen Riggs left as Assembly Hall director in 1997 for a similar position at the Schottenstein Center, in Columbus, Ohio, he took one of Champaign-Urbana's best with him. "I hired John as our first stage manager," Riggs recalls. "I'm very proud of John. He has been very successful and it has been great fun for me to watch him grow that company [John's company, Pagetech Limited]."

Xen Riggs appreciates the Assembly Hall even more in the years since he left Champaign. Riggs worked at the Assembly Hall from 1990-97 and became the director in 1994.

"I'm not sure the people of Champaign-Urbana realize what a pioneering facility the Assembly Hall was," Riggs says. "Between 1963 and 1987, it was one of the most remarkable facilities in the country. It was the first multi-purpose arena to do

Xen Riggs was the director of the Assembly Hall from 1994-97. Photo courtesy of the Assembly Hall.

theater, concerts and basketball. Now, that's the norm. . . . When I think of the Assembly Hall, the thing that jumps out, to this day, is seeing the iconic monolith rise out of the prairie. It's still awe-inspiring to me, particularly when you drive in from the South and see it rise out of the corn fields. That's pretty special. I'm sure that's why people have struggled for the last 20 years with what to do with it. To replace that kind of iconic image is tough."

Riggs had a background in entertainment as a booking agent prior to joining Wayne Hecht's staff. "One of the first things Wayne said, the first day I started was, 'I want something really big brought in,'" Riggs recalls. In his first year, Riggs pulled off a coup. He worked a deal to get the University of Illinois as one of three midwestern stops on Frank Sinatra's brief tour. Sinatra, nearly 75, played at the Assembly Hall on November 1, 1990, accompanied by a 35-piece orchestra.

Tickets for seats in the first six rows at Champaign were $100 apiece, "at the time, that was unheard of," Riggs says. Other floor tickets were priced at $45 each. The top four rows of C section were $17 apiece.

Sinatra's show was his first downstate since he hit the big-time in the early 1940s. At the time of his Assembly Hall appearance, he was listed in the Guinness Book of World Records for performing to the biggest crowd ever to attend a show by a solo performer, 175,000 people in 1980 at the Maracana Stadium in Rio de Janeiro.

The bar had been established at a high level. After the show, Hecht had a brief message for Riggs. "Do it again," Riggs says, remembering the conversation.

In 1991, Riggs started working on scheduling Billy Joel. "It was a campaign we worked at for three years," Riggs said. Joel agreed to appear (and did so on October 28, 1994), though it was the smallest community on his tour. His agents weren't optimistic. "They thought we'd lose money," Riggs relates. "The day tickets went on sale, they were great. The next day, his agent called and said they didn't have any idea it would do that well and there's no way we would have gotten him for that price if they did."

The entertainment business can be as exasperating as it is enjoyable. "There are high highs and low lows," Riggs says. "It's a difficult business. There are so many different personalities, so many things that can go wrong. Meeting people like Sinatra makes it cool."

Two of the persons Riggs says are special to him are comedians Bob Hope and George Burns, who were among the acts he signed up to play in Champaign. "Comedians tend to be a little more social," Riggs says. "Bob was one of the first acts I booked [for the Assembly Hall]. Bob could be intense at times. I worked with him over a five-year period. I learned when he started humming, that was his signal to be left alone. He wanted to get into work mode."

"George [Burns] was so genuinely nice and had a lot of energy for an older guy. The only persnickety thing about him was if you were eating in a restaurant and his soup wasn't hot, he'd send it back, but he never had a cross word for anyone."

Riggs wasn't afraid to push the envelope and take chances. Less than six months after he was the choice from 40 candidates nationwide to be the third permanent Assembly Hall director, he scheduled the Andrew Lloyd Webber and Tim Rice musical "Joseph and the Amazing Technicolor Dreamcoat." To get the show (from November 7-12, 1995), Riggs had to commit to eight performances. "We weren't sure how it would work," he says. "We didn't know how far people would travel." The Assembly Hall was partitioned off to a 3,600-seat theater and Riggs says, "it was one of our all-time successes."

His idea of a good night, he said, is easy to describe. "For me, it's when you walk out the night of the show and it's a full house and people are having fun," he says. "That's what we live for. You feel like you're contributing to the quality of life for people in the community." While in Champaign-Urbana, Riggs enjoyed a plethora of good nights.

By Melissa Merli with Fred Kroner

Members of the band KISS pose with Assembly Hall staff. LEFT TO RIGHT: Peter Criss, Sue Walker, Gary O'Brien, Gene Simmons, Kevin Ullestad, and Paul Stanley. Photo courtesy of the Assembly Hall.

9
The Thrill of Live Events

Kevin Ullestad, the current Assembly Hall director, has what sounds like the ideal job. He gets to book the entertainers and shows that perform at the facility. You'd think, as the person in charge, he could wrangle a front-row seat when the big-time acts hit Champaign-Urbana.

However, what is an evening of relaxation and pleasure for thousands is another night on the job for Ullestad, who (as of 2013) has been at the Assembly Hall 15 years. He may get the chance for a quick meet-and-greet — and has been photographed with the likes of Cher, Kiss and REO Speedwagon — but he mostly has to hear about the concerts and Broadway productions from others.

"I'm catching bits and pieces," Ullestad says. "If I catch three or four songs, that's good."

Going after the big acts

At one time, the Assembly Hall had a monopoly on attracting shows outside of Chicago or St. Louis. There were no other venues in the state with the seating to draw the popular acts.

Then, Springfield's Prairie Capitol Convention Center made its debut in 1979. The Rosemont Horizon opened in 1980, as did Danville's Palmer Arena. Peoria opened its 12,000-seat Civic Center in the downtown area in 1982. The Quad Cities finished its 12,000-seat arena (then known as The MARK) in 1993, and Bloomington's 8,000-seat U.S. Cellular Coliseum made its grand debut in 2006.

The bottom line is that Ullestad and his colleagues have to be proactive. That means not waiting for an agent or a promoter to make contact first. "With the increased competition, we're all chasing the same hook," Ullestad says. "We are chasing them. We have to be active.

"It has changed since the early days with Tom [Parkinson, the first Hall director] when JAM Productions [based in Chicago] brought shows to him."

One advantage for Ullestad is the stature of the building where he works. "Our reputation is still very strong," he says. "When it comes to the touring industry, we're very relevant. We have an incredible legacy and a building that is known throughout the Midwest.

"Some of the new, upstart acts don't appreciate the value of the building, but it is still an iconic facility. We run it as a professional business and have an incredible team that produces shows and promotes shows."

Serving many audiences

As the Assembly Hall prepares to celebrate its 50th birthday, Ullestad is one of 43 full-time employees (more than double the number of full-timers when the building opened). There are more than 600 part-timers on the payroll.

"We're like a small city when an event happens," Ullestad says. "There might be 15,000 people (in the stands) and 200 to 300 employees working.

"The key to our operation is our staff. They're a blessing to everything we do." Depending on the size of an incoming show, Ullestad estimates that as many as 60 to 70 stage hands could be working on a given day.

"We have to load the show in, produce it and load the show out," Ullestad says.

The number of events at the Assembly Hall fluctuates, but Ullestad estimates it's in the neighborhood of 100 annually. The rough breakdown is about one-third each for basketball games, national touring shows (whether concerts or Broadway productions) and university or community-related events such as graduations, trade shows, business expos or the Home and Garden Show.

"We serve the community," Ullestad says. "We're all about

LEFT TO RIGHT: Gary O'Brien, Cher, and Kevin Ullestad in the back hallway at the Assembly Hall. Photo courtesy of the Assembly Hall/Adam Babcock.

LEFT TO RIGHT: Scott Gelman, promoter, Tom Hamilton, Kevin Ullestad, Steven Tyler, Ray Tabano, Joey Kramer, Gary O'Brien and Joe Perry during one of Aerosmith's stops at the Assembly Hall. Photo courtesy of the Assembly Hall/Adam Babcock.

the diversification factor. We've served many, many audiences."

During Ullestad's time on campus, the yearly number of Assembly Hall visitors has generally stayed between 450,000 and 550,000.

Ongoing changes keep up with the times

When the Assembly Hall was constructed, the final price tag came out to $8.5 million. A 17-month backstage renovation (designed by FWAI Architects, Inc., from Springfield) which started in May 1997 and finished in October 1998 — after Ullestad had taken over the directorship — totaled $12 million. Like the original building, the funds were generated through student fees.

The renovation not only enticed Ullestad, a Des Moines native, to leave Iowa, but also proved invaluable with the Assembly Hall continuing to attract the entertainers and performances that fans are clamoring to see.

"The tours that are coming now are bringing eight, nine or 10 [semi] trucks," Ullestad says. "With a single-loading dock, they wouldn't look at Champaign." The renovation created three new truck tunnels and loading docks, as well as sparkling accommodations backstage in the downstairs (now air-conditioned) dressing rooms, a bigger dining room and expanded storage areas from approximately 4,000 square feet to the current 20,000 square feet.

"That kept us relevant," Ullestad says.

Fifty years ago, few folks imagined speaking on a telephone not attached to a cord or doing research on a computer instead of at the local library.

It stands to reason, then, that the next half-century will bring many more mind-blowing changes. Ullestad, however, believes one form of entertainment will remain untouched. "Even with all of the social media that's out there, live concerts will never go away," he says. "There's nothing like the rush when the lights go down and the first cords of the guitar are heard. There's electricity . . . I get a huge thrill out of the live event."

Depending on the act, Ullestad might be working on scheduling two years in advance (such as for Broadway productions). He has also put a show together in as little as a month's time.

Though his personal preferences are for classic rock 'n roll along with hot country, he leaves his bias out when booking shows. He strives for variety in order to appeal to a wide-ranging and diverse audience. "We go event to event to event and try to appreciate them all when they're here," he says.

At some point in the history of the venerable building, most of the nation's elite performers have played at least one show at the Assembly Hall. The Beatles never made it (though Beatle lookalikes, Beatlemania, appeared on November 1, 1980). Another person who has yet to appear — she's prominent on Ullestad's wish list — is Madonna, though she was as close as you can get without actually playing at the venue. She was one of the performers in Willie Nelson's 1985 Farm Aid Concert across the street at Memorial Stadium.

For Ullestad, a successful show or performance is one where the audience leaves with smiles on their faces and joy in their hearts. His day may not end until the lights are dimmed, but when he reflects there's no shortage of memories.

He tries to make himself visible when the stars arrive. "On occasion, I try to do a backstage meet-and-greet and present them a welcoming gift and thank them for including Champaign on their tour," he says.

He has learned to not try and anticipate what to expect from one show to the next. "Some acts will stay in the building longer than others," Ullestad says. "We have some great dressing rooms for their home away from home, but sometimes they don't stop in. They go from the bus to the stage."

The veteran administrator has found country stars such as Kenny Chesney and Rascal Flatts to be "very gracious," because "they value their fan base."

The Rascal Flatts trio played at the Hall on December 3, 2005, a few months after the magical 2004-05 men's basketball season when Illinois went to the NCAA championship. Rascal Flatts contacted Ullestad in advance with a special request. "They wanted game jerseys," recalls Ullestad, who accommodated the wish.

Among the others who've made a favorable impression with the director for being "very likeable and very talkative," he says, are Keith Urban and Fleetwood Mac, featuring Stevie Nicks.

Attendance records

Records, the saying goes, are made to be broken.

One Assembly Hall mark, however, has stood the test of time for more than three decades and may not be challenged any time soon. The single-event attendance record for an entertainer was established on Oct. 22, 1976 — the bi-centennial year — when 17,177 folks flocked to the Hall

LEFT TO RIGHT: Live Nation promoter Brian O'Connell, Rob Beckhom, Rascal Flatts band members Jay DeMarcus, Joe Don Rooney and Gary LeVox, Jennifer Larson, Kevin Ullestad and Live Nation promoter Scott Gelman at the Assembly Hall. Photo courtesy of the Assembly Hall.

LEFT TO RIGHT: Jennifer Larson, Carrie Underwood and Kevin Ullestad backstage at The Assembly Hall, October 2, 2008. Photo courtesy of the Assembly Hall/Adam Babcock.

to watch the King of Rock 'n Roll, Elvis Presley. Tickets were $12.50 apiece, generating more than $214,000 for the night.

Assembly Hall director Kevin Ullestad thinks that mark will be the standard infinitely, but not because the current stars don't have the drawing power. "The record will probably hold," Ullestad says, "because Elvis had a smaller stage. They didn't have the massive stages like they do now."

Kenny Rogers is the performer who has appeared on stage most frequently (10 times) followed by Alan Jackson and hometown heroes, REO Speedwagon (eight apiece).

The entertainment event that drew the most crowds over its lifetime was the now-defunct Ice Capades. In 30 years, covering 155 shows, the ice event attracted 1,093,510. Next in rank is one of former Assembly Hall director Tom Parkinson's pride and joys, the Ringling Bros. Barnum & Bailey Circus. The show was in town 17 different years for 107 performances, drawing 447,647 spectators.

A record that wasn't possible during the Assembly Hall's first 40 years of existence became reality in 2010. That spring, beer and alcohol sales were permitted at select events for the first time. When country star Jason Aldean made a February 4, 2012, appearance, alcohol sales at the concert exceeded the total revenue from the Hall's first fiscal year. With 15,000 fans in attendance for the Aldean show, beer and wine sales totaled $103,176. By contrast, alcohol sales for the entire 2010-11 school year amounted to approximately $96,000 or almost 10 percent of the $1 million on concession sales for the same time period.

The single-event record crowds for non-sporting events at the Assembly Hall are as follows:

EVENT	DATE	CROWD
Elvis Presley (tickets sold out in 6 hours)	Oct. 22, 1976	17,177
Johnny Cash	Oct. 4, 1969	17,040
Herb Alpert	Nov. 19, 1966	16,997
REO Speedwagon	April 21, 1981	16,622
Phish	Nov. 8, 1996	16,535
Def Leppard	Oct. 16, 1988	16,606
Garth Brooks	Sept. 11, 1992	16,544
Garth Brooks (all three nights were listed as sell outs)	March 7-9, 1997	16,500
New Kids on the Block	Nov. 8, 1990	16,500
U2	Oct. 22, 1987	16,500
Bob Hope	Oct. 21, 1967	16,378
Dave Matthews Band	Dec. 14, 2002	15,937
Jason Aldean	Feb. 4, 2008	15,128

For those musical artists that have played the Hall multiple times, the career-record crowds are as follows:

NAME	SHOWS	TOTAL ATTENDANCE
Kenny Rogers	10	88,869
REO Speedwagon	8	72,012
Garth Brooks	4	65,535
Alan Jackson	8	57,616
Alabama	6	55,313
Bob Hope	4	54,466
Chicago	5	54,438
Dave Matthews Band	4	47,227
Phish	3	45,569

Stevie Nicks of Fleetwood Mac in concert at Assembly Hall on May 9, 2004. Photo courtesy of *The News-Gazette*/Darrell Hoemann.

Assembly Hall Directors

NAME	YEARS
Tom Parkinson	1961-1987
Wayne Hecht	1988-1994
Eugene Barton*	1994-1995
Xen Riggs	1995-1997
Susan Maul*	1997-1998
Kevin Ullestad	1998-present

Interim directors while search was ongoing.

By Melissa Merli with Fred Kroner

Nashville twin giants John Jankowski and Roger Stieg at the 1978 Class A tourney. Photo courtesy of *The News-Gazette*.

PART THREE

THE ILLINOIS HIGH SCHOOL ASSOCIATION'S HISTORY AT THE ASSEMBLY HALL

Patrick Hatter (24) and Charles Claggett (32) teamed up to help Madison defeat Dunlap in the 1981 IHSA boys basketball championship game 58-47 on March 14, 1981. Photo courtesy of *The News-Gazette*/John Dixon.

10
IHSA Boys Basketball

The Illinois High School Association state boys' basketball tournaments were an Assembly Hall staple for 33 years. There were unbeaten teams that achieved their crowning moment of glory at the Hall, as well as future Olympians, future professional players and Hall-of-Fame coaches who spent at least one weekend of their lives in the arena.

There were underdogs who won and favored teams who lost. There were games in the old one-class system before the two-class format was introduced. There were games before the three-point shot was a reality. The games were memorable because the teenagers playing in them had reached the pinnacle of success at the high school level: a berth at state in the UI Assembly Hall.

One of the biggest Cinderella stories was written in 1964, the second year the Assembly Hall served as the IHSA tournament host. Tiny Cobden, with its 147 students, advanced all the way to the championship game, where it lost 50-45 to Pekin, a school with 2,726 students.

In the spring of 2012, former Cobden coach Dick Ruggles, then 75, remained proud of the precious memories from an era when the state crowned one — and only one — state champion per sport. "I'm still hearing stories about what we did," Ruggles says.

His 32-3 team upended seventh-ranked Galesburg, 60-57, in the quarterfinals and followed up with a 44-38 conquest over fourth-rated Stephen Decatur in the semifinals. His unranked team lost in the finals to number 8 Pekin.

Ruggles brought his team from southern Illinois to Champaign a day early so they could get over the awe of the huge surroundings in which they would play. "Some had seen Huff Gym, but this was an eye-opener," Ruggles recalls. "The conversation was, 'How many bales of hay would it hold?' The boys wanted to go to the top to see how small the floor looked from there."

Ruggles had his own message for the players. "Don't worry about all the seating," he reflects. "The floor is just a little bigger [than typical high school courts]."

Jim Neal, a senior in 1964, enjoys reliving the scene as the team bus pulled into the Assembly Hall parking lot. "I remember thinking, 'It looked like the explosion of the Atomic Bomb, the mushroom cloud effect,'" Neal says, "but those thoughts paled in comparison to the thoughts I had upon looking at the enormity of the inside . . . Being country kids, we had all spent hot, humid summer days hauling hay and filling some rather large barns with bales of hay. The thought of filling that place (with hay) was picturesque and frightening."

Though the state tournament experience was the highlight of his prep career, which concluded with nine points in the title game, Neal was pleased Cobden didn't play and practice at the site. "I remember trekking to the top row thinking, I'm glad we do not work out here, because running the bleachers in our little gym was bad enough. This place would kill us, knowing Coach Ruggles would certainly have used that option."

One area in which the Assembly Hall has drawn criticism — for the fans being removed from the action — is one that former Teutopolis head coach Ken Crawford grew to appreciate.

"The Assembly Hall was a great place to coach because the crowd noise did not interfere with players' ability to hear the coach while on the floor," Crawford recounts. "I found this very helpful to me in my attempt to communicate with my players. The players may not totally agree that this was an advantage to them."

Crawford's top-rated Class 1A 1986 team was unbeaten and captured a state crown. "My favorite memory," says Crawford, "came when I looked up at the Assembly Hall scoreboard in 1986 and it read 0:00. The championship game was over. All the pressure of going undefeated had thankfully ended and I looked into the

The 1984 McLeansboro Foxes celebrate winning the IHSA Class 1A boys basketball championship. They defeated Mount Pulaski 57-50. Photo courtesy of *The News-Gazette.*

St. Anthony's Scott Kabbes (20) chases Providence's Trennis Curry in a 1978 Class A consolation game. Photo courtesy of *The News-Gazette*.

Linn Arbogast (21) and Dave Harlan (33) from Dunlap in the Class A championship final game of Madison vs. Dunlap on March 14, 1981. Photo courtesy of *The News-Gazette*/Curt Beamer.

Scott Meents (44) from Herscher prepares to shoot over defenders from Flanagan in the 1981 Class A quarterfinals. Photo courtesy of *The News-Gazette*/Curt Beamer.

crowd to find my wife, who was smiling even though she was overdue with our first child."

Although diminished crowd sounds were helpful personally, Crawford understands what it means in the bigger picture. "Many venues are so loud that the players really can't hear the coaches," Crawford says. "This, however, also comes with a caveat. The crowd noise is definitely a part of high school and college basketball. . . . The acoustics of the Assembly Hall somehow muffle this noise and excitement. The Orange Krush has helped to correct this problem for the Illini. Our games at Carver Arena, in Peoria, were much louder and more like a high school atmosphere than when we played at the Assembly Hall in the Elite Eight."

Wheaton vs. Effingham's Chuck Keller (21) on March 20, 1981. Photo courtesy of *The News-Gazette*/Robert K. O'Daniell.

Pana vs. Liberty's Jeff Owen (34) on March 13, 1981. Photo courtesy of *The News-Gazette*/John Dixon.

William Nixon (52) and Eric Brown (30) of Westinghouse in their matchup against Wheaton on March 21, 1981. Photo courtesy of *The News-Gazette*/Robert K. O'Daniell.

This photo, released by the Illinois High School Association, shows announcer Tom Stocker standing on a bucket to interview 6-foot-8-inch Jack Sikma of St. Anne High School during the Illinois High School Association's 1973 State Finals. Sikma played 14 years in the NBA and won a championship with the Seattle Super-Sonics. (AP Photo/IHSA)

"Unfortunately, due in part to the move to the four-class system in high school basketball imposed by the IHSA Board of Directors in 2008, crowds have fallen off to a pitiful number and it now sounds like a funeral home at Carver," Crawford says. "While some favor a move back to Champaign, I fear the games would have the sound of a cemetery at midnight and the crowds would look like a mid-January New York Yankees fan rally at Busch Stadium [in St. Louis]."

Rantoul native Sean Taylor grew up watching games at the Assembly Hall and dreamed of one day playing there, but settled for the distinction of coaching Shelbyville at state the last year the Hall served as the IHSA host. "Even though we lost to Rock Island Alleman [in 1995], I still have vivid memories of coaching a game in a place where I watched so many games," says Taylor, a 2012 IBCA Hall-of-Fame inductee. "Every one of my players told me that the best memory of that season was walking out of the tunnel onto the Assembly Hall floor. . . . Sixteen years later, they still tell me that it was one of the greatest experiences they have ever had."

The cycle has gone full circle for Taylor, the Quincy High School head coach. When he has a night off, he joins his children at Illini games. "Now I get to relive those memories when I take my children to games at the Assembly Hall," Taylor says. "They are wide-eyed as they take in all that is going on around them. "My favorite new memory is from 2008 when I took my 4-year-old son, Kyle, to his first game at the Assembly Hall. With over 16,000 fans donned in orange, he leaned over to me during a second-half timeout and asked, 'How long after this game will the varsity game start?'"

High School basketball All-Stars and beyond

Think of the great players who have had the chance to play basketball at the Assembly Hall as high schoolers. From the thousands, the short list of basketball all-stars would include Mark Aguirre, Quinn Buckner, Kevin Garnett, Jay Shidler, Jack Sikma and Isiah Thomas.

One of the most successful prep point makers was someone with less name recognition that had the good fortune of playing on teams that were superior enough to qualify for state three consecutive years. Schlarman Academy boys' basketball coach Gary Tidwell started on teams coached by his step-father, Charlie Strasburger, and excelled once he suited up in Champaign.

Tidwell established the all-time — and still unbroken — record for Class 1A career free throw accuracy at state. In 12 games covering three seasons, he hit 89.3 percent of his free throws.

Tidwell's dream started at a young age after the transplanted Tennessean started living in Illinois. "As a son of a high school basketball coach, I have made many trips to the Assembly Hall both as a player and as a spectator," Tidwell says. "We moved to Illinois from Tennessee when I was in junior high, so my first impression of the building was the unique design from the outside that resembled a type of spaceship. . . . On the inside, it was the first arena I observed a game in and I was mesmerized by the number of people observing the game. Every year my dad would take the team to observe the Class 1A state tournament. It was at these moments that I caught the vision to one day play on the same floor that the Fighting Illini played on."

Tidwell's first chance came in 1988 as a sophomore at Pana High School. He didn't have to wait long for more opportunities. As a junior and senior at Fairbury's Prairie Central High School, he made two more trips to the Elite Eight.

The first time was special, Tidwell reflects. "The tournament directors allowed us to walk on the floor the Thursday evening before the Friday quarterfinal, and I was taken back on how far the bleachers were from the court," Tidwell says. "I remember standing at the free throw line and thinking this shot felt like a layup and then stepping back to the top of the key and thinking this shot felt like a free throw because of the depth perception from the basket to the bleachers."

In 2006, Tidwell was featured on the IHSA's list of the 100 Legends of the Boys' Basketball State Tournament, an elite team that helped the state organization celebrate the first 100 years of the state finals.

Fifty seven high school boys' basketball teams won their state titles at the Assembly Hall. The first nine were captured in the old one-class setup and the final 48 were during the period of the two-class system, which was abandoned in favor of a four-class event after the IHSA relocated the tournament to Peoria in 1996.

In all, 41 different boys' high school teams celebrated first-place finishes at the Hall. Pekin was the first with two championships (1964, 1967). Dolton Thornridge (1971, 1972) was the first to win in back-to-back years. Lawrenceville was the first with three state crowns in Champaign (1972, 1974 and 1982) as well as the first with four, adding its final title in 1983.

IHSA memories

Bondville's Bob Apperson had a tenure few can surpass. For 45 years, he was an Assembly Hall usher.

"When I first started, I worked every event they had," Apperson says. The Assembly Hall was 2 years old when Apperson's ushering career took hold. He was 29. He retired shortly before his 74th birthday in 2009.

Apperson enjoyed the state basketball tournaments, an annual staple for more than three decades at the Hall. He was especially appreciative of the concerned administrators. "The principal at East St. Louis Lincoln would tell us, 'if any of my students or fans give you a hard time, let me know and I will take care of it,'" Apperson relates.

He remembers the high school cheerleaders: "some were real bashful," he says, but their demeanor would change when they got into their mascot's uniform. "They'd go out there and make a fool of themselves," Apperson says.

When he was courtside, he made sure only those who were authorized reached the floor. "After the championship game, we'd let the principal on the floor for the ceremony," Apperson says. "One time, a gentleman came right behind the principal and I said, 'No, you don't.' He said he was his security."

Danville's John Spezia, president of the NJCAA men's basketball coaches association, was a senior starter on the first Bismarck-Henning team to win a regional championship (1968). The reward was that he and his teammates received tickets to attend the state finals. "It was a special time as hundreds of other high schools did the same thing, thus you saw hundreds of players like yourself in their letter jackets all across the Assembly Hall," Spezia says. "Rarely was there an empty seat."

A year later, Spezia played at the Assembly Hall. "Our Danville Junior College team played Parkland College before a University Illinois varsity game," Spezia recalls. "It was an exciting experience to come out of the tunnel, be in the locker room and actually play on the Assembly Hall floor."

It was the start of a lengthy relationship with the facility for Spezia. By the late 1970s, he saw games while recruiting for Valparaiso University and that opened the door to becoming a staffer at Lou Henson's annual summer basketball camps. "That led to a long friendship with assistant coaches Dick Nagy, Mark Coomes and Mark Bial, which led to the opportunity several times to watch practice and games at the Hall courtside," Spezia says. "Fond memories," Spezia says, "from varsity athlete to college player to high school coach to college coach and to a fan."

Mike Koon, who formerly worked in the sports information department at the University of Illinois, held courtside seats for many of the home Illini games. As a native of Monticello, he grew up as a basketball enthusiast, particularly high school state tournament games played in the building.

"Watching the likes of Art Kimball and Frank Bussone broadcast the state finals on television made young fans feel that the Assembly Hall was the epicenter of sports for that weekend," Koon says. "Getting to the Hall was a motivating force for teams all across the state.

"I remember Gibson City coach Jack Cowgill putting the image of the Assembly Hall on the back of warm-ups to define the Greyhounds' goal. That was the case for players from Rockford to Cairo."

Koon and his father were regulars at the annual tournament, starting in the early 1980s. "Some of my favorite memories were Bruce Douglas's nearly three-quarter court shot to lead Quincy to third place in Class AA in 1982; the battle of Bill Braksick [Flanagan] and Marty Simmons

[Lawrenceville] in the 1983 Class 1A final; number 1 Pinckneyville rolling through number 2 Watseka and number 5 Walther Lutheran only to be upset by Charlie Strasburger and Pana by four points in the 1988 Class 1A final; East St. Louis Lincoln and Peoria Central's epic three-overtime thriller for the 1989 Class 2A championship; and Thornton, coached by Rocky Hill and his purple suit, knocking off Kevin Garnett and top-ranked Chicago Farragut in the Class 2A quarterfinals of the 1995 tournament."

Koon's favorite Illini home game was the January 22, 1989, win by the Flyin' Illini over Georgia Tech in two overtimes. "The place was electric during the overtimes," Koon says. "I still have a shirt with Dick Vitale on it that says, 'No. 1 Baby,' that was sold afterwards."

IHSA BOYS BASKETBALL STATE CHAMPIONSHIP GAMES AT ASSEMBLY HALL
1963 — Carver (28-5) 53, Centralia (32-2) 52
1964 — Pekin (30-3) 50, Cobden (32-3) 45
1965 — Collinsville (30-2) 55, Quincy (26-6) 52
1966 — Thornton (30-2) 74, Galesburg (27-3) 60
1967 — Pekin (31-2) 75, Carbondale (29-3) 59
1968 — Evanston (30-1) 70, Galesburg (27-3) 51
1969 — Proviso East (30-1) 58, Peoria Spalding (28-4) 51
1970 — LaGrange Lyons (31-0) 71, East Moline United (30-3) 52
1971 — Thornridge (31-1) 52, Oak Lawn (30-3) 50
1972 Class 1A — Lawrenceville (25-8) 63, Mounds Meridian (30-2) 57
1972 Class 2A — Thornridge (33-0) 104, Quincy (28-5) 69
1973 Class 1A — Ridgway (32-1) 54, Maple Park Kaneland (20-12) 51
1973 Class 2A — Chicago Hirsch (29-2) 65, New Trier East (21-5) 51
1974 Class 1A — Lawrenceville (30-3) 54, Ottawa Marquette (29-4) 53
1974 Class 2A — Proviso East (29-4) 61, Chicago Heights Bloom (30-3) 56
1975 Class 1A — Venice (32-2) 65, Timothy Christian (27-6) 46
1975 Class 2A — Chicago Phillips (32-1) 76, Chicago Heights Bloom (23-10) 48
1976 Class 1A — Mount Pulaski (29-2) 59, Oneida ROVA (28-3) 58
1976 Class 2A — Chicago Morgan Park (28-5) 45, Aurora West (30-3) 44
1977 Class 1A — Madison (29-3) 71, Aurora Central Catholic (23-10) 55
1977 Class 2A — Peoria Central (29-2) 72, Springfield Lanphier (28-5) 62
1978 Class 1A — Nashville (30-3) 54, Havana (29-4) 38
1978 Class 2A — Lockport Central (33-0) 64, Westchester St. Joseph (31-2) 47
1979 Class 1A — New Lenox Providence (32-1) 46, Havana (31-1) 33
1979 Class 2A — Maine South (31-1) 83, Quincy (32-1) 67
1980 Class 1A — Luther South (27-5) 56, Peoria Bergan (23-8) 51
1980 Class 2A — Chicago Manley (31-1) 69, Effingham (30-2) 61
1981 Class 1A — Madison (30-2) 58, Dunlap (28-5) 47
1981 Class 2A — Quincy (33-0) 68, Proviso East (28-5) 39
1982 Class 1A — Lawrenceville (34-0) 67, Monmouth (31-2) 53
1982 Class 2A — East St. Louis Lincoln (29-1) 56, Chicago Mendel (29-3) 50
1983 Class 1A — Lawrenceville (34-0) 44, Flanagan (30-1) 39
1983 Class 2A — Springfield Lanphier (30-3) 57, Peoria Central (28-4) 53
1984 Class 1A — McLeansboro (35-0) 57, Mount Pulaski (29-3) 50
1984 Class 2A — Chicago Simeon (30-1) 53, Evanston (32-1) 47
1985 Class 1A — Providence St. Mel (31-3) 95, Chrisman (28-5) 63
1985 Class 2A — Chicago Mount Carmel (28-4) 46, Springfield Lanphier (29-4) 44 (2 OT)
1986 Class 1A — Teutopolis (33-0) 82, Ohio (29-3) 45
1986 Class 2A — Chicago King (32-1) 47, Rich Central (31-2) 40
1987 Class 1A — Venice (29-3) 56, Okawville (29-7) 54
1987 Class 2A — East St. Louis Lincoln (28-1) 79, Chicago King (28-5) 62
1988 Class 1A — Pana (28-3) 62, Pinckneyville (32-3) 58
1988 Class 2A — East St. Louis Lincoln (28-4) 60, Chicago St. Francis de Sales (29-2) 52
1989 Class 1A — Carlyle (32-3) 65, Rock Island Alleman (24-8) 56
1989 Class 2A — East St. Louis Lincoln (29-4) 59, Peoria Central (32-1) 57 (3 OT)
1990 Class 1A — Trenton Wesclin (30-3) 83, Prairie Central (31-1) 78 (2 OT)
1990 Class 2A — Chicago King (32-0) 65, Chicago Gordon Tech (30-2) 55

1991 Class 1A — Pittsfield (28-6) 45, Seneca (27-5) 35
1991 Class 2A — Proviso East (32-1) 68, Peoria Manual (31-3) 61
1992 Class 1A — Findlay (31-2) 61, Normal University High (29-4) 45
1992 Class 2A — Proviso East (33-0) 42, Peoria Richwoods (30-3) 31
1993 Class 1A — Staunton (27-4) 66, Hales Franciscan (23-11) 62
1993 Class 2A — Chicago King (32-0) 79, Rockford Guilford (27-7) 42
1994 Class 1A — Pinckneyville (33-2) 67, Eureka (30-2) 65
1994 Class 2A — Peoria Manual (27-6) 61, Carbondale (28-4) 60
1995 Class 1A — Normal U-High (29-3) 56, Aurora Christian (32-2) 54
1995 Class 2A — Peoria Manual (32-2) 65, Harvey Thornton (30-2) 53

Jamie Brandon of Chicago King in a game against East St. Louis, March 17, 1990. Photo courtesy of *The News-Gazette*/Robert K. O'Daniell.

Laphonso Ellis rebounds the ball in the 1988 IHSA State Tournament at the Assembly Hall in Champaign. Photo courtesy of *The News-Gazette*.

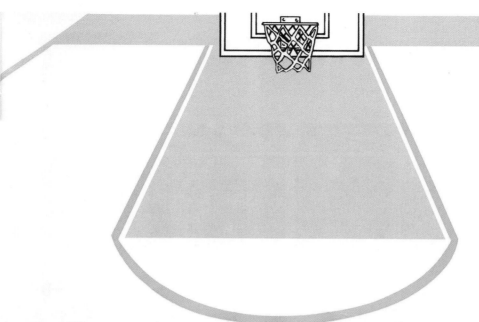

ILLINOIS

Class A & Class AA Girls

9th State Final Tournament ● 6th Year of 2-Class Series

ASSEMBLY HALL ● CHAMPAIGN, ILLINOIS ● MARCH 28-30 ● $1.50

11
IHSA Girls Basketball

During the 14 years the Assembly Hall served as host for the girls' basketball state tournament, 26 titles were won. The first two came during the era when one state champion was crowned and the last 24 occurred during the time there were state titles awarded to the small-school and the big-school winners.

Only three schools secured more than one title in Champaign. Quincy Notre Dame was the first to win twice at the Hall (1983, 1984). Chicago Marshall and Teutopolis each annexed four championships. Both high schools won their third titles in 1989 and their fourth in 1990.

There were also three high schools that celebrated titles in Champaign in both boys' and girls' basketball: East St. Louis Lincoln (one girls', four boys'), Peoria Manual (one girls', two boys') and Teutopolis (four girls', one boys').

The all-time girls' state tournament scoring leader, 1990 Ms. Basketball Courtney Porter, from Hume Shiloh, played state games at the Assembly Hall each year during her prep career. Her teams finished with four state trophies.

Shiloh's Courtney Porter established the all-time girls' state tournament scoring record (regardless of class) following

Wheaton's Yvonne Simmons, left, attempts to regain control of the ball after Chicago Marshall's Sheryl Porter, right, knocked it loose during the 1985 Class AA championship game in Champaign. Chicago Marshall won by a score of 63-37. Photo courtesy of AP/Seth Perlman.

Doris DeBerry (5), of Chicago Marshall, demonstrates her unique free throw form in the 1984 IHSA class AA tournament. Photo courtesy of *The News-Gazette*/John Dixon.

Chicago Marshall coach Dorothy Gaters is in tears after winning the 1982 IHSA Class AA Girl's basketball tournament on March 27, 1982. Marshall defeated East St. Louis Lincoln 57-49 to take the title. Photo courtesy of AP.

RIGHT: Elmhurst York's Patti Smalley (54) carries Pam Fiene (21) as they clebrate their 55-46 victory over Peoria Richwoods to capture the 1984 IHSA Class AA girls basketball championship in Champaign. Photo courtesy of AP/Seth Perlman.

Rick Atterberry and former Illini women's basketball star Kendra Gantt broadcast the 1985 IHSA girls basketball championships from the Assembly Hall. Photo courtesy of *The News-Gazette*/Brian K. Johnson.

Altamont's Deb Culver (10) tries to drive around Eldorado's Ronda Ego (32). The Eldorado Eagles defeated the Altamont Indians 79-57 in the 1981 Class A IHSA girl's basketball state quarterfinals. Photo courtesy of *The News-Gazette*.

Kathy Bradford of Massac County is consoled by her father, Melvin Bradford, after she pulled a muscle coming off the floor prior to her semi-final Class A girl's game vs. Seneca. She has a stuffed animal in her hands. Photo courtesy *The News-Gazette*/Brian Johnson.

Maple Park of Kaneland, coached by Rick Shairer, celebrates its 1981 Class A victory over Metropolis of Massac County in the championship game. Photo courtesy of *The News-Gazette*/John Dixon.

Chicago Marshall coached by Dorothy Gaters, celebrates its 1981 Class AA victory over East St. Louis Lincoln in the championship game. Photo courtesy of *The News-Gazette*/Robert K. O'Daniell.

her senior season. In the 12 state games she played at the Hall from 1987 to 1990, Porter scored a total of 241 points for an average of 20.1 points per game.

The run of the girls' ISHA tournaments ended in style with Sullivan's nationally ranked 1991 team concluding its 35-0 season with the final three wins coming at state.

"The best memory," center Becky Clayton Anderson says, "was walking through the tunnel of the Assembly Hall for that first game. What a sense of awe. Emerging from that tunnel to the sea of red and black from Sullivan was something I will never forget. . . . I was saddened to hear the girls' state tournament was not going to be at the Hall after

Members of the 1991 Sullivan Class A IHSA state championship girls basketball team reunited in the gym at Sullivan High School in Sullivan on Tuesday, February 7, 2006. Standing from left are: Misha Coy, Amanda Glazebrook, Becky Clayton, Tiffinie French, Sheri Adams and Stephanie Monroe. Front from left are coaches Scott Thomas and Dave Van Deursen. Photo courtesy of *The News-Gazette*/John Dixon.

that year, but, in a way, I'm glad we were the last girls' team to win the championship there. The Assembly Hall has a majestic feel to it that cannot be described unless you have played on the floor. To run the court and imagine the many that have run on it, too, made our undefeated season even that much more special."

Sullivan point guard Amanda Glazebrook had experienced the Assembly Hall from the spectators' point of view, but that couldn't compare to being in on the action. "Playing on the same floor as the Illini, getting to use their locker rooms and sitting on the benches where they did was such a thrill, but the ultimate was running out of the tunnel with your team and hearing the roar of the crowd yelling for your team. The 'Go Red' cheer spreading throughout the Hall was as cool as hearing the I-L-L and I-N-I cheer."

IHSA GIRLS BASKETBALL STATE CHAMPIONSHIP GAMES AT ASSEMBLY HALL

1978 — Joliet West (29-2) 64, Lincoln (24-3) 48
1979 — Niles West (28-1) 63, East St. Louis Lincoln (32-2) 47
1980 Class 1A — Benton (25-6) 52, Sidell Jamaica (23-2) 42
1980 Class 2A — East St. Louis Lincoln (31-0) 64, Chicago Marshall (30-3) 47
1981 Class 1A — Chicago Christian (31-2) 44, Quincy Notre Dame (28-4) 36
1981 Class 2A — Elk Grove Village (31-1) 50, Peoria Richwoods (30-2) 33
1982 Class 1A — Maple Park Kaneland (32-1) 55, Massac County (21-5) 41
1982 Class 2A — Chicago Marshall (32-0) 57, East St. Louis Lincoln (28-3) 49
1983 Class 1A — Quincy Notre Dame (30-0) 57, Rushville (29-3) 53
1983 Class 2A — Peoria Richwoods (32-0) 56, Chicago Maria (28-3) 43
1984 Class 1A — Quincy Notre Dame (30-2) 56, Teutopolis (28-1) 53 (OT)
1984 Class 2A — Elmhurst York (32-1) 55, Peoria Richwoods (31-1) 46
1985 Class 1A — Elgin St. Edward (29-4) 48, Teutopolis (28-4) 46
1985 Class 2A — Chicago Marshall (30-1) 63, Wheaton Central (29-3) 37
1986 Class 1A — Teutopolis (31-1) 59, Massac County (30-2) 44
1986 Class 2A — Peoria Manual (27-3) 57, Chicago Marshall (29-4) 46
1987 Class 1A — Seneca (30-0) 54, Carthage Hancock Central (30-1) 47
1987 Class 2A — Westchester Immaculate Heart of Mary (32-2) 45, Massac County (29-4) 43
1988 Class 1A — Teutopolis (32-0) 54, Elgin St. Edward (29-5) 35
1988 Class 2A — Des Plaines Maine West (35-0) 46, Elmhurst York (29-6) 37
1989 Class 1A — Teutopolis (31-1) 46, Shiloh (30-1) 44
1989 Class 2A — Chicago Marshall (29-2) 56, New Trier (32-3) 50 (OT)
1990 Class 1A — Teutopolis (30-1) 62, Nashville (29-3) 29
1990 Class 2A — Chicago Marshall (27-5) 65, Aurora West (30-3) 49
1991 Class 1A — Sullivan (35-0) 65, Seneca (28-1) 48
1991 Class 2A — Chicago Mother McAuley (31-3) 69, East St. Louis Lincoln (28-2) 65

The News-Gazette's 1991 All-Area girl's basketball posed for a group photo at The Assembly Hall. FRONT ROW, LEFT TO RIGHT: Traci Butler, Chrisman; Tami Engel, Gibson City; SECOND ROW: Martina Underwood, Clinton; Amber Pierce, Hoopeston-East Lynn; Nicki Bryant, St. Joseph; THIRD ROW: Dana Eisenmenger, Unity; Melanie Ward, Prairie Central; Gayle Tate, Georgetown-Ridge Farm; Becky Clayton, Sullivan; and Amanda Glazebrook, Sullivan. Photo courtesy of The News-Gazette/Curt Beamer.

WRESTLING

1995 boys individual
STATE TOURNAMENT
58th Year of State Series—22nd Year of Class A and AA

Saturday, February 18
Site: Assembly Hall
University of Illinois • Champaign, Illinois

IHSA
Illinois High School Association

Official Program (Saturday Edition) $3.00

12
IHSA Wrestling

After Illini men's basketball, the longest running athletic event in the Hall is the IHSA state wrestling tournament. The annual event celebrated its 40th consecutive year at the Hall in 2012, and its 43rd appearance overall at the site. The IHSA put the Assembly Hall in a rotation with Northwestern and Illinois State University before Champaign became the full-time tournament host. The wrestlers first competed at the Assembly Hall in 1967 and returned in 1969 and 1971 before it became a fixture in 1973, the final year of the one-class tournament.

According to Rob Sherrill, who authored *Mat Madness: 60 Glorious Years of Illinois High School Wrestling* in 1996, the inaugural state finals at the Assembly Hall provided some unique twists. "It was a Cinderella finish to an improbable season that saw Rock Island become the only sub-.500 team ever to win the state championship. Rock Island started the season 1-5 in dual meets, and needed a season-ending three-match winning streak to pull their final record to 6-7," Sherrill reported. "The Rocks then finished fourth in the district and fourth in the sectional."

Team scoring at state was determined solely by the performance of a school's qualifiers, not by a separate dual-team tournament, which was established in 1984. Rock Island's 1967 squad had two athletes reach state and both of them made their way to championship matches. Don White was

Jim Flynn of IHSA, 1984. Photo courtesy of *The News-Gazette.*

1984 tournament. Photo courtesy of *The News-Gazette.*

From right, Assembly Hall attendants Paul Clifton, Travis Dees, Mike Burke and Derrick Marion roll out a wrestling mat on the floor of the Assembly Hall on February 13, 2008. The Assembly Hall was preparing for the IHSA State Wrestling Tournament. Photo courtesy of *The News-Gazette*/John Dixon.

The state meet continues with action on multiple mats. Photo courtesy of *The News-Gazette*/Robert K. O'Daniell.

1984 tournament. Photo courtesy of *The News-Gazette*.

1992 tournament. Photo courtesy of *The News-Gazette*.

Aaron Rathbun (Prairie Central) wrestles against Gabe Boatman (Vandalia) in class A at 145 pounds at the IHSA wrestling tournament in 2003. Photo courtesy of *The News-Gazette*/Robert K. O'Daniell.

Wrestlers practice on a Thursday afternoon at the Assembly Hall. Photo courtesy of *The News-Gazette*/Robin Scholz.

140-pound Kyle Dooley, Monticello, beat Eric Celletti, Byron, in a championship bout at the IHSA Wrestling Tournament at the Assembly Hall in 2007. Photo courtesy of *The News-Gazette*/Robert K. O'Daniell.

1992 tournament. Photo courtesy of *The News-Gazette*.

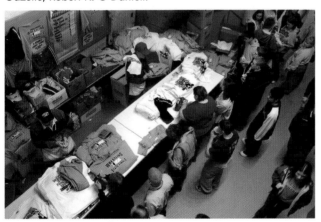

Customers wait in a long line to purchase IHSA Wrestling State Tournament t-shirts at the Assembly Hall in 2004. Photo courtesy of *The News-Gazette*/Heather Coit.

the 145-pound champion and Carl Moore was the runner-up at 127 pounds. White was the only one of the 12 individual weight-class champions that year to win by pin.

Another 'first' occurred when the Assembly Hall served as wrestling host for the first time: the IHSA implemented a fifth-place match. That winner earned a medal, however the sixth-place finisher was not then considered a medalist. This did not change until the IHSA instituted a two-class tournament in 1974. From 1941 (the fifth year for the state wrestling finals) through 1972, only the top four finishers had been awarded medals.

Before the Assembly Hall was awarded the state finals for its decades-long run, the tournament already had a longstanding history in the community. The first five IHSA wrestling state finals were held at the UI's West Stadium Hall, underneath the west stands at Memorial Stadium. It then shifted to the Men's Old Gym Annex from 1942-1948 (with no tournament in 1944) before heading to Huff Gymnasium in 1949.

MOST STATE CHAMPIONSHIPS, CAREER

4, Mark Ruettiger, New Lenox (Providence), 1978A (98), 1979A (112), 1980A (119), 1981A (126)

4, Joey Gilbert, Tinley Park (Andrew), 1986AA (126), 1987AA, (132), 1988AA, (132), 1989AA (135)

4, Mike Mena, Sterling (Newman), 1989A (112), 1990A (119), 1991A (125), 1992A (125)

4, Joe Williams, Chicago (Mt. Carmel), 1990AA (135), 1991AA (152), 1992AA (153), 1993AA (160)

4, T.J. Williams, Chicago (Mt. Carmel), 1993AA (135), 1994AA (140), 1995AA (145), 1996AA (145)

4, David Douglas, Chicago (Luther South), 1994A (112), Dolton (Thornridge), 1995AA (119), 1996AA (130), 1997AA (135)

4, Chase Beebe, Lombardi (Montini), 2000A (103), 2001A (112), 2002A (125), 2003A (130)

4, Conor Beebe, Lombard (Montini), 2002A (103), 2003A (112), 2004A (125), 2005A (125)

4, Mike Benefiel, Lombard (Montini), 2004A, 2005A, 2006AA (152), 2007AA (171)

4, Albert White, Chicago (St. Rita), 2004AA (135), 2005AA (140), 2006AA (145), 2007AA (152)

4, Seth Milks, Dakota, 2006A (103), 2007A (112), 2008A (119), 2009 1A (130)

MOST WINS, CAREER

CLASS 1A: 13, Nick Harrison, Stillman Valley, 3 at 112 in 2008, 4 at 119 in 2009, 3 at 119 in 2010, 3 at119 in 2011

CLASS A: 13, Trevor Elliott, Sandwich, 3 at 103 1989, 4 at 112 in 1990, 3 at 119 in 1991, 3 at 119 in 1992

CLASS AA: 18, Mike Poeta, Highland Park, 5 at 103 in 2001, 5 at 119 in 2002, 4 at 140 in 2003, 4 at 152 in 2004

COMBINED: 16, David Douglas, Luther (South), 4 at 112 in 1994A; Dolton (Thornridge), 4 at 119 in 1995AA, 4 at 130 in 1996AA, 4 at 135 in 1997AA

Parents and fans lined up outside the Assembly Hall to get tickets to the 2004 IHSA State High School Wrestling Championships. Photo courtesy of *The News-Gazette*/Vanda Bidwell.

MOST WINS, TOURNAMENT

CLASS 1A:

4, John VanDuyne, Wilmington, 135, 2009

4, Nick Harrison, Stillman Valley, 119, 2009

4, Cameron Vance, Port Byron (Riverdale), 125, 2009

4, Seth Milks, Dakota, 130, 2009

CLASS 2A:

4, Chris Williams, Bethalto (Althoff), 119, 2009

4, Ryne Harris, Belleville (Althoff), 112, 2009

CLASS 3A:

4, Edwin Cooper, New Lenox (Providence), 112, 2009

4, Curtis Blaydes, Chicago (DeLaSalle), 285, 2009

4, Zach Smith, Rockford (Boylan), 215, 2009

4, Mario Gonzalez, Aurora (West), 189, 2009

4, Lee Munster, Fox Lake (Grant), 171, 2009

4, Kyle Czarrnecki, Buffalo Grove, 160, 2009

4, Bobby Barnhisel, OakPark (Fenwick), 152, 2009

4, Elias Larson, Chicago Hts.(Marian), 145, 2009

4, Matt Bogess, Mt. Prospect (Prospect) 140, 2009

4, Kevin Fanta, Lake Zurich, 135, 2009

4, Nick Dardanes, Oak Park.(O.P.-River Forest),130, 2009

4, Jameson Oster, Lockport (Twp.), 119, 2009

4, Eddie Klimara, New Lenox (Providence), 103, 2009

4, Tony Ramos, Carol Stream (Glenbard North), 125, 2009

CLASS A:

4, by 141 wrestlers

CLASS AA:

6, Rob Bearce, Pekin, 112, 1979

6, Dan Evensen, Marist, 98, 1983

6, John Massa, East Moline (United), 119, 1987

6, Mike Poloskey, Joliet (Central), 275, 1987

6, Dion Simmons, Decatur (MacArthur). 160, 1990

6, Eric Siebert, LaSalle (L.-Peru), 1991

6, Micah Hey, Dixon, 125, 1994

6, Michael Murdough, St. Charles, 140, 1994

6, Tony Opiola, Chicago (Mt. Carmel), 135, 1998

6, Sam Kuntz, Chicago (DeLaSalle), 171, 2002

6, Tyler Williams, Carol Stream (Glenbard North), 140, 2002

6, Pat Castillo, LaGrange (Lyons), 125, 2003

Lou Henson and Deon Thomas. Deon averaged 18 points in four seasons for the Illini. Photo courtesy of The Assembly Hall.

PART FOUR
ILLINI BASKETBALL FINDS ITS HOME AT THE ASSEMBLY HALL

Photo courtesy of The Assembly Hall.

Circa 1960s.
Photo courtesy
of the Assembly Hall.

13
The Early Days of Illini Basketball in the Hall

Dave Downey remembers having mixed emotions about the Assembly Hall. Sure, the grand opening was highly anticipated. The prospect of playing in the state-of-the-art facility was one of the appeals when athletes in the UI's Class of 1963 were recruited as high schoolers. "They said we would play in it when we were sophomores," Downey recalls. "It got done when we were seniors." Former teammate Bill Small recalls it well. "We were supposed to have three years," Small says, "and we got two games."

Completion of the structure took much, much longer than plans had indicated. Downey, Small and their classmates were down to the final two home games of their collegiate careers when they got the green light. That's when the reservations surfaced. "At that time, because we were trying to win the Big Ten [title], we were not particularly anxious to move," Downey says. "The seniors would have been happy to finish at Huff Hall. It was a great place to play."

Huff, built in 1923, created an intimate atmosphere as spectators lined the court. Capacity was such (6,700 persons) that only about 4,000 students per game were in attendance and they were limited to three games per season in 1956 so others could see the games in person. "People had to move their feet to let us throw the ball in-bounds," Downey remembers.

Of all his years playing basketball, Small believes the loudest crowd was for the farewell at Huff on February 23, 1963, a game in which the Illini overcame a halftime deficit to beat Wisconsin. "Huff was fantastic," Small recalls. "Fans were 3 feet from the end lines. The most noise I ever heard at a game was in our last game at Huff. The Chief was there and danced at halftime."

The Illini had one 90-minute practice at the Assembly Hall before christening the court with a March 4, 1963, game against Northwestern. The 8 p.m. game was a sellout (16,137), but there was not a home-court advantage for Illinois. "It was like everyone was in awe," Downey says. "We didn't play particularly well. The baskets were tight. Shots would hit and bounce off."

"I made the first basket," Downey says, with a smile, "when we went there to practice." It was understandable, Downey believes, why the teams had difficulty shooting. "It wasn't just there," Downey says. "We didn't play in domes and the [shooting] background was very tough. There were no other big multi-purpose facilities. We played in field houses and old gyms. No one in the Big Ten, other than Ohio State, had a dedicated basketball arena. Rupp Arena [in Kentucky] was not built yet."

Dave Downey. Photo courtesy of *The News-Gazette*.

Dave Downey with his old basketball hoop and the ball from the 1963 NCAA tournament in his home in Champaign in 2011. Photo courtesy of *The News-Gazette*.

The Illini scored a win over Northwestern, 79-73, and five days later added one over Iowa, 73-69, which completed an 11-0 season sweep of home games. The final two triumphs, Downey contends, were attributed to one thing. "We were better than Northwestern and Iowa, and we beat them," he says. "It was nice to be a part of it, but it was not that big of a deal at the time."

Statistically, at the Assembly Hall the Illini were unable to match the level of play they'd exhibited earlier in the season at Huff Gym. Illinois' first four home conference games all at Huff ended with coach Harry Combes's team scoring at least 90 points. Despite the point drop-off, the 1962-63 Illini still finished second in the conference in scoring (87.2 average) for Big Ten games. The 1962-63 Illini, ranked eighth in the final national Associated Press poll, was Combes's final 20-win team.

The Assembly Hall — both upstairs and downstairs — was strikingly different than it is as the 50th anniversary approaches. "It was the floor and two baskets," Small says. "There were no bleachers behind the baskets. Just the two benches were on the court. It was like going to a neutral court." It was in the first year of the Harv Schmidt coaching era (the 1967-68 season) that he requested the installation of seats on the floor and increased the capacity by 1,200 seats.

The players' changing rooms were not fully furnished when Downey and Small christened the building. While the players kept their focus on the task at hand, everyone else was caught up in the historical implications of the moment. "In the community and around the country, it was a really big deal," Downey says. "This was the first [venue] of its kind."

Small, an Aurora West graduate, is proud to have been part of the first group to use the Assembly Hall. "That was one of the inducements, when we were seniors in high school," he says. "They had a nice model in a display case and said it would be ready our sophomore year. Back then, freshmen weren't eligible [to play in varsity games] and we were told we would be the first group in there. "We were, but it wasn't until the end of our careers."

Box score of the first game

Illinois 79, Northwestern 73

NORTHWESTERN (8-15)

NAME	FG	FT	TP
Phil Keeley	4	5	13
Rick Lopossa	6	7	19
Bill Woislaw	1	1	3
Marty Riessen	2	0	4
Rich Falk	3	1	7
Don Jackson	0	2	2
Bill Gibbs	3	11	17
John Miller	2	2	6
Ken Lutgens	0	2	2
Totals	21	31	73

Coach: Bill Rohr

ILLINOIS (18-5)

NAME	FG	FT	TP
Bob Starnes	2	3	7
Dave Downey	6	7	19
Bill Burwell	4	4	12
Tal Brody	3	10	16
Bill Small	5	9	19
Skip Thoren	0	2	2
Bill Edwards	1	0	2
Bogie Redmon	1	0	2
Totals	22	35	79

Coach: Harry Combes

Halftime: Northwestern 36, Illinois 33.

Attendance: 16,137

Photo courtesy of the Assembly Hall.

Photo courtesy of the Assembly Hall.

Firsts in the Assembly Hall

Danville Commercial-News sportswriter Fowler Connell, who was still covering Illini basketball during the 2012-13 season at age 89 as part of the WDAN radio crew, kept track of numerous firsts when Illinois opened the Assembly Hall on March 4, 1963. Following are some of the observations he shared with readers of his newspaper in the March 5th edition.

MILESTONES

First rebound: Dave Downey, Illinois

First Illini shot: Bill Small, Illinois

First foul: Bill Burwell, Illinois

First Illini point: Bill Burwell (at 17:49)

First Illini basket: Dave Downey (at 16:38)

First three-point play: Tal Brody, Illinois (at 13:41)

First tie: 26-26 on a Dave Downey free throw (at 14:47)

First official's timeout: At 15:32 for a loose shoe

First Illini lead: 37-36 on a Bill Burwell rebound (at 19:01 of second half)

First lost child: At 4:45 of second half

First win: Illinois, 79-73

Scott Spitz defends against Deon Thomas during practice on February 8, 1991. Photo courtesy of *The News-Gazette/ Delfina Colby.*

Read all about it

On March 4, 1963, the doors were open and greeters stood by much earlier than was the custom for home Illini men's basketball games. At 5:45 p.m. on opening night, the first of the spectators were entering the building.

The idea was to alleviate traffic jams as well as to provide ample time for the curious to take a sightseeing tour before taking their seats. There was even a warm-up game with the UI freshmen basketball players taking on the UI freshmen football players 2 hours prior to the 8 p.m. start of the main event.

In the minutes leading up to the inaugural varsity tipoff, Everett Kisinger directed his 110-piece UI band. Sportswriters were present, taking note not only of the action, but also of the reactions of the sideline observers. The game stories were not typical of the era.

Photo courtesy of the Assembly Hall/Mark Jones, U of I Sports Information.

Danville Commercial-News sports columnist Fowler Connell offered this account.

CHAMPAIGN — It was tremendous! Beautiful! Fabulous!

The Assembly Hall, to be sure. Not Illinois' weary basketball forces which had to scrape, struggle and free throw their way past Northwestern (79-73) in the debut at their new basketball home.

Sixteen thousand, 137 persons must have agreed to the man that there isn't a finer basketball setting in the world.

And probably another 16,000-plus would agree with both coaches that it "wasn't a particularly good game."

But when the final cheers had died down (and there's no echo to deafen you in the Assembly Hall), Illinois found itself right back where it started — a full game back of pace-setting Ohio State.

The Illini figured to get past Northwestern (and they came close to letting it get away). They had hoped for some help from Minnesota. They didn't get it.

So now the Illini must dispose of Iowa Saturday in their early afternoon game in the Assembly Hall. Then they will gather around the TV set to cheer for Indiana (whoever heard of Illinois boys cheering for Hoosiers?) in the later afternoon TV contest against Ohio State.

If Illinois should beat Iowa (a likely situation) and Indiana and Mr. Rayl should upset Ohio State (an unlikely event), the Big Ten basketball race would end in a tie. And Illinois will get the chance to play in the NCAA tournament since Ohio State was the last team to represent the conference and would be ineligible to go under the present rules.

In postgame interviews, UI players Dave Downey and Bill Small let it be known they were not enamored with the Assembly Hall.

"This isn't a particularly good place to shoot," Downey was quoted. "You have to hit everything dead center or it (the ball) will come out."

Small spoke to the same theme: "You could be a bit off in Huff and the ball wouldn't bounce out," he said.

Larry Harnly, then a senior at the UI and a staff correspondent for the *State Journal-Register* in Springfield provided this view.

CHAMPAIGN — Coaches Bill Rohr of Northwestern and Harry Combes of Illinois agree on at least one thing: There will be better basketball games played in the new Assembly Hall here than the one that initiated the new palace Monday night.

"It was a new place and both teams were anxious. It was not a good game," said Combes after Illinois' 79-73 triumph.

"Neither team played as well as they did in the first game (between the schools). Maybe they were tired," said Rohr. "The best team won the game." Illinois won the first game at Northwestern 78-76 on Bob Starnes' 55-foot field goal in the closing seconds.

"We didn't do badly on defense, but we couldn't get our offense in gear. The baskets seemed a little rigid," Combes said.

Dave Downey was as proud of his record as a predictor as he was of his new school career scoring record.

"I predicted before the game that neither team would shoot over 40 percent," the star forward said. He was right. Illinois sank 22 of 61 field goal tries for a record of 36.1 percent.

Illinois' Cory Bradford lays the ball up past Wisconsin's Dave Mader after a steal late in the first half on Wednesday, January 23, 2002. Photo courtesy of AP Photo/John Dixon.

Deon Thomas on March 10, 1991 during an Illinois vs. Indiana game. Photo courtesy of *The News-Gazette.*

Kiwane Garris drives around Missouri's Jason Sutherland Photo courtesy of *The News-Gazette*/Mark Cowan

Northwestern made 21 of 70 for 30 percent.

Downey tied and broke the former school record of 1,299 (points) set by Johnny Kerr, now with the pro Syracuse Nets, when he sank two free throws with 5 minutes, 13 seconds left in the first half.

Writing for the hometown *News-Gazette,* sports editor Ed O'Neil penned the following.

Illinois launched the mammoth, magnificent Assembly Hall to the tune of a nail-biting 79-73 victory over Northwestern Monday night, but the chances for a Big Ten title slipped one notch further away.

A crowd of 16,137 came to cheer the home forces, marvel at the spectacular building and listen to the serenading of a 110-piece band.

But shabby play on both sides, provoked no little by two added musical starters performing a duet on whistles, made it something less than a rousing sendoff for the Hall.

The basketball was very ordinary, the officiating was the same.

While the two teams were hitting 43 field goals — the odd one to the Illini — the referees mistook the largest crowd ever to see a game in the state outside of Chicago as a welcoming committee for striped clothing.

They called 57 personal fouls and turned the evening into a march in the waltz tempo from one end of the floor to the other. Those fouls resulted in 88 free throw attempts — more than two a minute — of which 66 found the mark.

The gunners should have been so accurate from the floor. Their shooting was no better than the officiating.

Finally, in the *Champaign-Urbana Courier,* Vern Richey offered this observation: "The lights had been on before, but tonight electricity came to the Assembly Hall."

Although the Assembly Hall immediately became the home court for the men's basketball program, throughout the first decade they had to pay to play. A story in the November 19, 1969, edition of *The News-Gazette* revealed a little-known arrangement. "Although it was originally recommended that the Athletic Association would not pay rental use for the use of the basketball team's home court, it has been charged $1,000 for each home game since 1963. In addition, it pays $25 per practice session, $250 to install the floor for practice. . . . Under a new agreement, entered into in June, 1969, the Athletic Association will pay the variable total of out-of-pocket costs, plus $500 per game in 1969-70, $600 per game the following year."

Paint the Hall Orange. Photo courtesy of the Assembly Hall.

14
Coaches and Staff Share
Their Unique Perspective

Lou Henson

Henson's first game at the Assembly Hall was a 76-54 exhibition win on November 21, 1975, against the University of Windsor (Canada). The listed crowd was barely 3,000. "Once the season was under way, we drew better," Henson recalls. "At the time I came, we hadn't been to the NCAAs in a number of years [12]. I didn't expect a lot of fan support early."

Henson's first official game at the Assembly Hall was a 73-54 win over Kent State on December 1, 1975. The attendance was 5,007.

Henson also recorded the 600th of his 779 collegiate wins at home (January 21, 1993) on the date that Penn State made its first-ever visit to the Assembly Hall. The Illini won, 82-66, before a crowd of 11,665 spectators.

The final home game of Henson's storied career was a loss in the National Invitation Tournament to Alabama, 72-69, in a March 13, 1996, game that drew 8,398 persons. It was at the regular-season finale a few days earlier (March 9, a 67-66 loss to Minnesota) that Henson took the microphone after the contest and announced his impending retirement.

"The Assembly Hall and the athletic department had worked together to dress up the Hall," then UI-trainer Rod Cardinal recalls. "It took me by surprise, and the crowd didn't know it would take place." Both Henson and his wife, Mary, were honored during the post-game ceremony.

Henson's overall 21-year coaching record at the Hall was 256-69, a winning percentage of 78.8 percent. His first Illini team had a 14-13 final record and his last team was 18-13 overall. He took the Illini to the NCAA tournament in his sixth year as coach and 12 times during his stint with the Illini, including a trip to the Final Four in 1989.

Fighting Illini men's basketball coach Lou Henson. Photo courtesy of the Assembly Hall.

Mark Coomes

Former Illinois assistant Mark Coomes calls the 1993 win over Iowa "an unbelievably dramatic game."

Not far behind, in his estimation, is the 103-92 overtime win on Super Bowl Sunday against Georgia Tech during the Flyin' Illini's 1988-89 march to the Final Four. "We went to number 1 [nationally] the next day," Coomes recalls, "but Kendall [Gill] broke his foot [in the first overtime, and missed 12 games]." Gill scored 19 points in the game. That win was the 17th in a row to start the season for the Illini, who suffered their first loss four days later at Minnesota.

Also prominent for Coomes was a January 26, 1976, verdict over 17th-ranked Michigan, 76-75. "That signified that Lou [Henson] was in the big leagues," Coomes recalls. "At that point, it was a signature win in his first year. That gave us the traction to get going and recruit and we got Levi [Cobb] and Eddie [Johnson]."

Coomes also cited the December 22, 1990, win over Louisiana State University (102-96) as a significant highlight. "The game we beat LSU and Shaq sticks out," Coomes says. "We had Scott [Pierce] guarding him and

Illinois vs. Minnesota at the Assembly Hall on Jan. 29, 2005. Illinois Beat the Gophers 89-66 and celebrated their 100th basketball season. Orange Krush members show their support for former coach Lou Henson. Photo courtesy of *The News-Gazette*/John Dixon.

Coach Harv Schmidt coached the Illini men's basketball team from 1967-74. Photo courtesy of the Assembly Hall.

Fighting Illini men's basketball coach Lou Henson. Photo courtesy of the Assembly Hall.

The crowd loved Lou Henson. Photo courtesy of the Assembly Hall.

Rennie [Clemons] half-dunked on him." Clemons drove the lane, elevated over Shaq and scored on a play where O'Neal was called for his fifth foul.

It would be easy to vote for the December 24, 1984, Illini game against the nation's second-ranked Kentucky Wildcats. The Christmas Eve game had 10,732 spectators. A Central Illinois blizzard prevented the scheduled officials from traveling to Champaign, so three referees were summoned from the stands and outfitted with the proper attire. Working the 56-54 Illini loss were Charlie Due, Bob Hiltibran and Bill Mitze.

Bruce Weber

Illinois' 2004 win over Wake Forest was a special win in a special Final Four year. "The thing I remember," former Illini head coach Bruce Weber says, "is we were up about 37-20 and referee Steve Welmer ran by, tapped me on the shoulder and said, 'Sit down, relax and enjoy it.'

"They had Chris Paul and were ranked number 1. We were number 3, but played about as well as we could ever play. After that, we were (ranked) number 1 and held it through the (NCAA) championship game."

Another fond memory for Weber at the Hall is of a game Illini fans would rather forget. It came in the 1980s when Weber was on Gene Keady's coaching staff at Purdue.

"Illinois had us down by 17 points — and this was before the shot clock — with about 8 minutes left, but did not score another basket and we won on a shot at the buzzer."

Even during his tenure in West Lafayette, Weber looked forward to away games at the UI Assembly Hall. "It was always fun," he says. "I have good memories of stopping at The Beef House [in Covington, Indiana] on the way over."

One return trip, however, was much less pleasant. It followed the January 21, 1984, Illini win (76-52) in the Assembly Hall. "After the ride home, Coach Keady had a practice at midnight, or maybe it was 1 o'clock in the morning," Weber recalls.

As for the Assembly Hall, current Kansas State coach Weber had a different perspective depending on from which bench he viewed the action. "As an assistant at Purdue, I remember the band and the electric guitar," he says. "Your bench was on that end and it would irritate you. The Krush would get after you pretty good. It was a pretty tough place to play," Weber recalls.

"As the head coach, you have them on your side and it was a tremendous advantage to play in the Assembly Hall. There were tremendous crowds and, despite the size and the high ceiling, it gets pretty noisy at times."

A milestone victory on the court in Weber's first year was also a milestone moment for the UI's marketing folks. The 75-51 blowout of first-place Michigan State on February 10, 2004, signified a successful start to the "Paint the Hall Orange" promotion. "Deron [Williams] said, 'We have to keep this Orange; it's so intimidating,'" Weber recalls. "We made the push and everyone seemed to buy in."

The crowd for the MSU game was a sellout 16,618 — one of eight Assembly Hall sellouts that season — and the fans saw James Augustine register a double-double (16 points, 11 rebounds).

Orange-clad fans became so prevalent that it was an issue Weber had to address in recruiting. "One recruit came in on a spring day, when there was a concert or something going on," Weber recalls. "[The building] was pretty gray. I told him, 'this is where we play.' He said, 'No, it's not. I've seen it on TV. Where you play is orange.' I had to tell him that's the image he sees from all of the orange worn by the fans."

Bruce Weber on the floor during an Illini game at the Assembly Hall on Sunday, February 26, 2012. Weber got a foul on the bench for being out of the coaches box. Photo courtesy of *The News-Gazette/* Robin Scholz.

Rod Cardinal, 2003. Photo courtesy of *The News-Gazette*/John Dixon.

Brian Cardinal in Tolono on September 16, 2011. Photo courtesy of *The News-Gazette*/Heather Coit.

Weber is one of four UI coaches to go through an entire home schedule without a loss. His 2004-05 team was 15-0. The first undefeated home season was by Harv Schmidt's 1968-69 squad (12-0). Lou Henson enjoyed two perfect home seasons (1984-85, 15-0, and 1988-89, 17-0). Two of Bill Self's teams ran the table at the Assembly Hall. His 2000-01 team was 12-0 and his 2002-03 team was 14-0.

Rod and Brian Cardinal

Rod Cardinal's job was one where he went to work hoping it wouldn't be a busy day. From 1973 until he officially retired (from full-time work, at least) in 2003, Cardinal was an athletic trainer for the University of Illinois. Nothing gave him greater pleasure than watching an event without being called on to check the condition of an injured athlete.

The toughest days at work were those when he was on the clock, but longed to be a fan—when his son, Brian, played basketball for Purdue University (1996-2000). Brian finished his career with the Boilermakers second on the all-time list for career starts.

"His first game [at Illinois] was his redshirt year [1995-96] when he was six months removed from the Assembly Hall," Rod Cardinal recalls. "He walked out of the tunnel and it was like a receiving line of people. He knew every usher. He knew every technician. He basically knew everyone by name."

When Brian Cardinal wasn't playing basketball for the Unity High School Rockets, he was spending time with his dad at the Assembly Hall. He was the ball boy for the Flyin' Illini's 1988-89 team which advanced to the Final Four in Seattle.

They are times that Brian Cardinal cherishes, even after completing his 12th NBA season in 2011-12. He treasures all the memories, even those that didn't include shooting baskets. "It was incredible, seeing my dad in action," Brian Cardinal says. "We'd get there early and I'd help him cut up oranges and watch as he taped ankles."

During the Flyin' Illini's memorable 1988-89 run, there was frequently a person exiting the tunnel on game day a few steps after Nick Anderson, Kenny Battle, Kendall Gill, Lowell Hamilton and company. "The chance to walk through the tunnel after the team and experience the jubilation of the fans was the coolest thing," Brian Cardinal recalls.

The youngster took seriously his role as the "sixth man"—that fan in the stands who hopes to make a difference in whether the home team wins or loses. "I always thought for one magical moment if I held my chin with one hand, the other team would miss their shot, and it was my way to help the team with my shenanigans," he relates.

The main thing that Brian Cardinal saw from his young eyes was the key to reaching the elite level as an athlete. "To be in their work environment, to see how hard they worked and everything that went along with being a college athlete, I knew that was what I wanted to do," Brian Cardinal says. "Essentially, the Assembly Hall is where my mind started wandering in terms of dreaming, and what I wanted to accomplish. It might not be the most glamorous place, but in my mind, it's one of the best. It was awesome."

Brian Cardinal grew up as a fan of Lou Henson and his long-time staff. "Since I could walk, I remember walking on the Assembly Hall floor," Brian Cardinal recalls. "Never officially being offered a scholarship was somewhat hurtful, but also understandable."

In retrospect, he realizes there would have been more than the hometown pressure from a fan base who'd scrutinized his high school career for years.

"Those guys [Henson and staff] are special people and I always wanted to play for those guys, but there'd be pressure on my father," he says. "What if someone was hurt at my position and didn't get back [cleared to play] as soon as some people thought . . . there's a variety of things I'm thankful we didn't have to deal with even though I had to change nearly half my wardrobe when I went to Purdue. . . . Everything I had was Orange and Blue."

"To have as many memories as I have, I'm obviously still an Illini fan," Brian Cardinal says. "Regardless of what happened, I'll always be a huge Illini fan."

UI coach Bill Self wears an orange coat on the sidelines at the senior day basketball game against Iowa in 2001. Photo courtesy of *The News-Gazette*/Robert K. O'Daniell.

Rod Cardinal has a memory bank full of Assembly Hall moments. "A neat event was after we returned from the Final Four in Seattle [in 1989]," Rod Cardinal says. "We knew something was planned, but we didn't know what. John Mackovic [then athletic director] got us organized outside. When we came in, someone had painted a yellow brick road on the floor and we had to follow the yellow brick road to the stage."

"The best thing ever was the 100-year celebration (Jan. 29, 2005)," Rod Cardinal says. "It was so spectacular to see those guys lined up in the tunnel, out of the tunnel and out the door to get introduced after the game [an 89-66 victory over Minnesota]."

"Colin Handlon [letterman from 1937-40] was the oldest guy [86, and he led the parade of former athletes]. He was so proud, I thought he'd burst out of his suit."

Rod Cardinal's expertise was occasionally required when entertainers were in town. "A cast member with Joseph and the Amazing Technicolor Dreamcoat sprained an ankle, but she said she had to perform that night," Rod Cardinal recalls. "I worked with her with ice, ultrasound, in the whirlpool and taped her up."

The dancer's thank you was two tickets to the evening performance. "My daughter and I went and after the show, when they came out for their bows, she pointed at me and gave a couple of claps," Rod Cardinal says.

With the hiring of John Groce as the UI men's basketball coach following the 2011-12 season, Rod Cardinal is now working under his seventh staff. His tenure started with Harv Schmidt and continued with Gene Bartow, Lou Henson, Lon Kruger, Bill Self, Bruce Weber and now Groce. "I help on a part-time basis," says Rod Cardinal, whose title is Director of Special Projects.

Photo courtesy of the Assembly Hall.

Kiwane Garris drives the ball as Roger Powell (43) defends during the Night of Legends' Alumni Basketball game in 2008 at the Assembly Hall. Photo courtesy of *The News-Gazette*/Holly Hart.

15
Playing in the Hall

Deon Thomas

Career scoring leader Deon Thomas has a special fondness for two home games. The first was the February 4, 1993, win over Iowa, 78-77. "The game against Iowa really stands out," Thomas says. "The whole thing with Iowa was very big and to pull out that game in the fashion we did was amazing. T.J. [Wheeler's] pass and Andy [Kaufmann's] shot [a three-pointer with 1.5 seconds remaining] was truly one of the best times for me in Assembly Hall."

The outcome helped to shake off more than the ghost of Bruce Pearl, the Iowa assistant who had alleged improper recruiting by Illinois after Thomas had committed. For Thomas, it meant a measure of redemption, "especially," he recalls, "after the go-ahead basket bounced off my shoulder."

Thomas's other standout moment came later in the calendar year. On December 11, 1993, he broke Eddie Johnson's UI record for career points scored as the Illini overpowered American University 108-84. He broke the mark with a first-half basket. "Being able to share that moment with my teammates and especially with my grandmother, Berniece McGary, is something I will hold forever in my heart," Thomas says.

Thomas finished his 118-game collegiate career with 2,129 points. Johnson (who now stands seventh) had 1,692 points.

Cory Bradford

"It has to be one of the loudest places in the country," former Illini Cory Bradford says. "I have so many memories in that building that I get goose bumps just thinking about it, just like I had during my Big Ten champions' reunion speech last summer [2011].

"Being in that place brings back so many great moments that I had in my four years. Boy was it a fun ride. It has a long history of great teams and so many wonderful moments that guys can think back on in their career and I bet 90 percent of them happened in the Assembly Hall."

Kiwane Garris

Former Illini Kiwane Garris holds the Assembly Hall in high regard. "I have been in many arenas and stadiums, but by far the Assembly Hall is one of the best in the world," Garris says. "It was a great place to play. The atmosphere was like being at home with family, having a house party. With family, friends, alumni and the student section, it was always loud in there. I loved running out of the tunnel when it was game time.

"I love when the cheerleaders started the I-L-L and then I-N-I chant. That let you know we were having a good time. Then, they did that race around the arena with the flags, one group of cheerleaders on the first level and another group on the second."

Garris was introduced to the Assembly Hall in advance of his enrollment. "My first time playing in the Assembly Hall, I was a junior in high school," Garris recalls. "I called it 'The Mushroom,' from the Smurfs. Never knew after that I would be playing in there for my college years."

Illinois' Cory Bradford passes against Minnesota at the Assembly Hall. Photo courtesy of *The News-Gazette/ Holly Hart.*

16
Sportscasters and More

Loren Tate

Loren Tate, 2011. Photo courtesy of *The News-Gazette*/Rick Danzl.

Few people — if any — have watched as many Illini games at the Assembly Hall as former *News-Gazette* sports editor Loren Tate. He was there for the opening game in 1963 — as a spectator who joined three buddies — and he was still there throughout the 2012-2013 season.

His perspective is that of a veteran scribe. "First," Tate says, "it should be understood that a multi-purpose building constructed a half-century ago doesn't stack up in basketball terms with modern basketball-specific structures. Such is the case with the Assembly Hall. It lacks in intimacy for basketball customers due to the wasted space at court level. And, the top row of Section C is much too distant. Nor are there the lucrative suites and boxes like you'll find at the majestic buildings in Chicago and Indianapolis, or at the Big Ten sites in East Lansing and Madison.

"In the latter cases, it was a simple and noncontroversial process to move out of old field houses and build new arenas. Not so at Illinois. The Assembly Hall is a unique and iconic structure that will be moving onto the National Registry of Historic Buildings, making it all the more untouchable. It doesn't make sense, based on Champaign-Urbana's population, to erect a comparable building alongside the one that is already there."

Loren Tate's recounts his favorite Assembly Hall memories, as follows:

- March 4, 1963: "For a guy who can't figure out why airplanes fly, you can imagine my uncertainty when I entered a structure that didn't have posts to hold up the roof. Arriving late, we were in such a hurry and so awestruck that we forgot where we parked the car, and had a terrible time locating it when we left the flying saucer."
- January 11, 1979: "The joint was jumping with TV cameras and wild-eyed fans as 15-0 Illinois rocked Magic Johnson and MSU's top-ranked Spartans, 57-55, on Eddie Johnson's late baseline jumper."
- February 4, 1993: "This game was lost. That's what makes Andy Kaufmann's shot so stunning. Iowa went ahead 77-75 and there wouldn't have been time for Kaufmann to convert T.J. Wheeler's long heave if precious fractions hadn't been put back on the clock. This outcome was all the more sweet because of the bad feelings that existed between the rival schools."
- December 1, 2004: "Illinoisans could smell this one coming for miles. Wake Forest's Deacons were number 1, and the Illini were poised to replace them. Despite being in foul trouble, Deron Williams dished out 11 assists as the home team built a 32-point lead and coasted 91-73 as part of a 29-game win streak. This game alerted a nation as to how good the Illini were."
- March 4, 2006. "It fascinated me the way Dee Brown was able to peak against Tom Izzo's MSU Spartans. He burned them for 54 points in two conference games in 2006, and was phenomenal in all aspects of a 75-68 regular-season finale. At his best, Brown was breathtaking and highly memorable."
- January 10, 2012: "Still fresh in the memory bank is the UI's 79-74 upset of number 5 Ohio State, because it was so unexpected and because Brandon Paul was able to cap a 43-point spree with a closely-guarded, high-difficulty trey in the closing minute."

Scott Eisenhauer

Scott Eisenhauer is best known as the mayor of Danville. Before that, he was a popular radio sports broadcaster in the community for WDAN. He started the announcing phase of his life at the grass roots level, as a 7-year-old at the UI Assembly Hall.

"My most memorable attempts at play-by-play will always be the large number of Fighting Illini basketball games I 'called' from Section C of the Assembly Hall, entertaining an audience of one,"

Eisenhauer says. "As a grade-schooler, my father (Harry) would take me to University of Illinois games whenever time and tickets were available. . . . Up to the top section of the Assembly Hall we would climb, waiting for the game to start. My father would always take a radio so he could listen along, occasionally sharing with me statistics or interesting facts about the two teams. One day, in a hurry to get to the Hall for a game, he forgot his radio and, not wanting my father to miss the opportunity to 'hear' the game while also watching it, I began to provide him with my version of play-by-play. While I realize now I was nowhere near as good as he usually listened to, he made it seem like I was the best he had heard," Eisenhauer recalls. "From that game on, for many games to come, he often 'forgot' his radio, giving me the assignment of providing him with the commentary on those Fighting Illini wins and losses. I will always consider the Assembly Hall as the place where I got my start in sports broadcasting and where my love for providing an audience with the play-by-play of an exciting sporting event was born and grew."

Jim Sheppard

Jim Sheppard, who had more than two decades as the public address announcer at home UI men's basketball games, had the privilege of being on the microphone for many Illini wins of significance.

Scott Eisenhauer, 2004. Photo courtesy of *The News-Gazette*/ Heather Coit.

He was there on January 12, 2005, when, after a 90-64 triumph over Penn State, Illinois became the 11th school nationally with 1,500 victories. He was there for Lou Henson's 600th win (January 21, 1993, 82-66 over Penn State), for Lon Kruger's 300th win (December 8, 1999, 98-61 over Texas Pan-American); for James Augustine's rebound to break the UI career record (held by Efrem Winters) on December 20, 2005, and for Bruce Weber's 200th win (December 3, 2006, 87-59 over IUPUI).

Sheppard's debut occurred on November 26, 1985, a night the Illini defeated Loyola, 95-64. "Before the game, as I was walking down the stairs toward the court level, an Assembly Hall security person asked who I was," Sheppard recalls. "After I replied, the person said, 'You have some big shoes to fill.' I always have remembered that because after I was gone in 2007, I had been the voice of the Assembly Hall longer than anyone."

Sheppard, who replaced Tom Trent as the Assembly Hall announcer, coined his famous "Deeeeeee for three" after one of the many three-pointers made by Dee Brown. He first said it on November 27, 2002, in a 96-43 Illini win over Arkansas-Pine Bluff. "Those sitting around me at the scorer's table were a bit surprised, but enjoyed it," Sheppard says. "I used the phrase for the rest of Dee Brown's career and it became one of my trademark phrases. T-shirts were made and to this day, fans still remember it."

Sheppard's list of memorable games is topped by the December 9, 2000, win over Seton Hall. "Illini play flat in the first half and trail 42-25 at the break," Sheppard recalls. "Coach Bill Self lashes out at guard Frank Williams in the locker room and that's all it took. Williams scores 17 in the second half and Illinois stages the greatest comeback in school history, resulting in an 87-79 overtime victory. In the OT, Cory Bradford — who sat on the bench the final 5 minutes of regulation — drilled a three-pointer, his first of the game, to tie the NCAA record for consecutive games with a three-pointer (73). Bradford wound up with a still-standing record of 88 straight games making a three-pointer."

Sheppard has proof that the Assembly Hall was a rockin' place when the Illini played at home. "The loudest ever," Sheppard says, "was January 23, 2007. The Illini hosted Indiana and [coach] Kelvin Sampson. Illini fans exploded into a sea of boos as Sampson emerged from the tunnel before the game.

Jim Sheppard. Photo courtesy of *The News-Gazette*.

The reason: recruit Eric Gordon going to the Hoosiers after announcing to play at Illinois. . . . Assembly Hall employee Doug Pugh, who handles the sound at the Assembly Hall, said the decibel level hit .105 with no band noise, on the calibrated meter. And Pugh was sitting in level B of the Assembly Hall." Illinois won the game, 51-43, before a sell-out crowd of 16,618.

Another of Sheppard's special moments occurred on February 6, 2001 in the game against Michigan State. "It was the number 4 Spartans vs. the number 7 Illini," Sheppard says. "If the Illini wanted to win the Big Ten championship that year, they had to take care of the three-time defending champions from East Lansing, Michigan. Dick Vitale was in town for the nationally televised game, but it was still a ticket-scalper's paradise. There was solid orange everywhere in the Hall. Cory Bradford connected on six three-pointers and the Illini won 77-66 in one of their most exciting games ever at the Assembly Hall."

Other UI games on Sheppard's list of all-time favorites (which were included in the 2007 book *Are You Ready?*):

- December 1, 2004 vs. Wake Forest: "The visitors were ranked number 1, but didn't impress the Illini. Illinois dominated the game and won 91-73. The Demon Deacons shot only 39 percent from the field against a solid Illini defense. Roger Powell Jr. led a balanced scoring attack with 19 points."
- February 13, 2001 vs. Wisconsin: "With 2.5 seconds to play and the Badgers holding a one-point lead, the Illini's 16-game home winning streak, their Big Ten title hopes and a chance for a number 1 NCAA tournament seed were all on the line. Illinois had the ball on its own baseline and Sean Harrington's inbound pass went to Marcus Griffin, who was under the basket and dropped the ball in with 0.8 seconds left on the clock. The Badgers threw a long pass the length of the court, which was intercepted by Frank Williams, and that was it. The Illini won 68-67."
- March 1, 1987 vs. Indiana: "Seniors Ken Norman, Doug Altenberger and Tony Wysinger score 24, 22 and 10 points, respectively, to lead Illinois to a 69-67 win against the number 3 Hoosiers. Indiana does not lose another game that season and captures the national championship, coach Bob Knight's third and last."
- January 28, 1991 vs. Iowa: "Illini legend Harold 'Red' Grange dies early in the day in Florida, the Middle East war continues and I announce for a moment of silence to remember our troops before tipoff. Uniformed police are positioned behind the Iowa bench and the tense feelings continue in the wake of the Deon Thomas-Bruce Pearl recruiting scandal. The Illini win 53-50."
- February 12, 1998 vs. Michigan State: "The Illini crush the Spartans 84-63 to move coach Lon Kruger's squad into a first-place tie for the Big Ten lead. Michigan State star Mateen Cleaves, who scored 27 points against Illinois earlier, was held to 11 points. The Illini finish the season tied for first in the conference, the first time they tasted a championship since the 1983-84 season."

Scott Nagy

Scott Nagy, coaching South Dakota State against Illinois at the Assembly Hall in 2005. Photo courtesy of *The News-Gazette*/Robin Scholz.

Scott Nagy had an Assembly Hall perspective unlike most. The son of long-time UI assistant Dick Nagy, he literally grew up in the building. Nagy later was a grad assistant with the Illini (1988-89 and 1989-90) and ultimately returned as a visiting head coach, bringing his South Dakota State squad to town on Nov. 18, 2005.

Though his Jackrabbits dropped a 90-65 decision, Nagy says, "Coming back as a head coach was very gratifying. Most people won't even remember the game, but it was important to me for so many reasons. It's a game I will always remember."

At the top of his favorite Illini moments is a game from the Flyin' Illini's 1988-89 season. "Beating Michigan [96-84 on January 14, 1989]," he says. "There was such a big buildup to the game and Coach Henson said we looked like a grade-school team next to them. There were about 10 pros on the floor and we just crushed them," he recalls. "Of course, this was followed by the incredible [overtime] game with Georgia Tech that vaulted us to number 1 [nationally]. We had just played them in the Rainbow Classic and they were an incredible team. Kendall [Gill] broke his foot and we hung on to win a very tough-fought game [103-92 on January 22, 1989]. It was as good of an atmosphere that I had ever seen in the Hall."

Nagy said it's interesting to see how perceptions — and perspectives — change with the years. "I remember when I was in eighth grade [1979-80] and the Illini went to the NIT Final Four," he says. "I think we beat Murray State [65-63 on March 13, 1980] to go to New York and I can remember someone had written a song about the team and the season. I laugh at that now because if they went to the NIT, they would be stringing the coach up."

Dave Shore

Dave Shore, a native of Paxton, Illinois, is a sportscaster who's had professional stops in Lexington, Portland, Dallas and — since December 2010 — Los Angeles. "Basketball arenas are my most favorite of venues," Shore says.

The UI Assembly Hall is among Shore's favorites. "Assembly Hall brings both an incredible rush and a great student section to make it one of the best for me." He says, "The building's construction and 'feel' makes up a large part of the atmosphere, but most importantly, it's the tradition and fans inside that make it the true great experience."

Shore first saw Illini games as a junior high student in Paxton. Far removed from the Orange Krush, he still reveled in the surroundings. "The school spirit and fight songs rising to the top of the roof made it an experience that just could not be felt watching on TV," Shore says. "Every home game is a true fan experience and, at Illinois, it has held its tradition over the years and the passing of the torch through so many eras of college students. . . . Illini fans can be very proud of the atmosphere they have created inside the Hall, but also the structure itself reeks of tradition in the architecture. You can build new arenas now, but you can't make them great sports atmospheres. Suites do not equal home court dominance.

"From a national sportscaster perspective, I truly believe that Assembly Hall is one of the best venues currently in collegiate sports."

Shore's job forced him to watch many memorable UI games on television, but he says "attending any game I could, no matter the importance, brought not only excitement, but also true school spirit and loyalty among young and old."

The Last Dance of Chief Illiniwek, portrayed by Dan Maloney, at the Assembly Hall on Wednesday, Feb. 21, 2007. Photo courtesy of *The News-Gazette*/Darrell Hoemann.

17
The Chief's Last Dance

Chief Illiniwek's halftime performances were a staple at the UI from 1926 through a men's basketball game on February 21, 2007. The following month, the UI Board of Trustees voted to retire the Chief Illiniwek name and his Sioux regalia.

"That was my last game as public address announcer at the Assembly Hall after 22 years," veteran PA personality Jim Sheppard says. "Dan Maloney as Chief Illiniwek performs for the final time, ending a remarkable 80-year tradition. There was a happy ending, as Illinois won 54-42."

In the following excerpt from *Chief Illiniwek: A Tribute to an Illinois Tradition,* Dan Maloney recounts his experience that night:

As I stepped onto the court at the Assembly Hall on February 22, 2007, I felt like the epicenter of a disorienting flood of light. I had an acute awareness of the 16,618 fans hanging on each tap of my toe against the hardwood, each twist of my wrist that made the soft rawhide fringe dangling off my regalia dance, but still I struggled to find my steps as an incessant flicker of flashbulbs rained down on the arena like silver foil confetti falling on a New Year's celebration. Despite my focus on the task at hand, the rug burn on my feet as I sprinted up the ramp was replaying in my mind.

I squinted beneath my handmade headband of colored beads and white rabbit fur, struggling to see the sea of florescent orange fans bidding Chief Illiniwek farewell. I could hardly find them as they pointed digital cameras and disposable ones, cell phones and handheld video equipment directly at my face—his face. I picked out my girlfriend, Catherine, standing a few feet in front of me, in line with center court. She had this pained smile that said she was proud of me but still felt utter sadness at the events that had transpired. Off to the side I could see my parents, brothers and sister gathered at the baseline. As I looked through photos and spoke to them in the months following that night, I can see the look of both sadness and pride, a strange dichotomy that can take anyone by surprise. I knew they were somewhat understanding of my emotional state over the past two weeks, but most of the masses of fans did not see me beneath the paint, the feathers, the deerskin chaps and tunic that composed an insignia they had watched dance this dance for almost 81 years.

Rarely did anyone from one of my worlds know who I was in the other. I'm not a famous kid; I don't have a famous face. Normally I'm not that distinguishable. Normally, I like being anonymous. Normally, I like being able to blend into a crowd. That all changed on Feb. 16, 2007, when Lawrence C. Eppley, chairman of the University of Illinois Board of Trustees, decreed the end of Chief Illiniwek. Chairman Eppley's announcement on that February morning was intended to signal the end of the Chief tradition. But it also began a new era in my college experience. While 35 Chief portrayers before me had shied away from the limelight, establishing the tradition of separating their public and private faces, I suddenly became the voice of one of the most controversial symbols in the world of college sports.

On that night of nights, Feb. 21, 2007, to say something was different is a simply an understatement. There was an impression of melancholy percolating through the air. I could feel it in my bones. When people came up to say hello or to ask if I could take a quick picture with them, nearly every single one of them had their eyes glazed over, desperately fighting back the inevitable tears that would flow during the Three in One. The emotions went beyond the surface. It was a glaze that covered and permeated everything in the Assembly Hall. I could see it in my parents' eyes, hear it in people's voices, and feel it as I walked back into the locker room after the performance, out of sight of message boards, online comments, protestors, supporters and fans.

Architect renderings of an updated Assembly Hall, both inside and outside.

CODA

What Lies Ahead for the Assembly Hall

For a brief time in 2004, it seemed unlikely the Assembly Hall might reach its 50th anniversary. A consulting design firm recommended without reservation that the most efficient course for the university to meet its future facility needs — particularly for basketball — was to demolish the iconic structure and build an entirely new arena.

Initially greeted as a practical solution by university leaders, the idea fell quickly under the weight of public outcry. The Assembly Hall, university leaders soon agreed, must stay. But to stay, the arena must be updated to meet current needs and fashions. So it was back to the drawing board as officials contemplated options that would preserve the current appearance of the Hall to satisfy public opinion, and simultaneously deliver myriad improvements inside. It was a challenging charge — and an expensive one.

By the time this history was written, the drawing board was full. A new generation of leaders in the University Division of Intercollegiate Athletics were looking at drawings and contemplating plans. But equally challenging, they were seeking donors to cover a price tag expected to exceed $165 million.

In his first year on the job at Illinois, new Athletic Director Mike Thomas received his first up-close, inside look at both the benefits and the challenges the building offered. "It's an iconic building, and what a great home-court advantage it is. I'm impressed. . . . It's a building that is very-well maintained. It has a great foundation and, in some ways, it's a great place to watch a game," Thomas said.

Before his hiring as the UI men's basketball coach in the spring of 2012, John Groce was familiar with the Assembly Hall from the perspective of a visiting coach. "I thought it was an intimidating environment," Groce says. "This and one other building were the two toughest in the league to play in terms of volume, excitement and energy."

But former Illini coach Bruce Weber was privy to some of to some of the shortcomings. "Ideally, you want something new if you're coaching there," Weber says. "The plans I'd seen six or seven years ago would have been a nice upgrade. It has been there 50 years. Do something, that's better than nothing, so it can stand another 50 years and our grandkids can walk in and feel proud of it."

Athletic director Thomas's vision is that it will become an even better place to watch future games. "We need to make it a 21st century facility," Thomas states.

The process of starting a facelift began with the February 2012 hiring of an architectural firm from Kansas City, AECom, which won the bid for the design of the $165-million-plus overhaul.

"The hope is we'll try to establish a conceptual design we can take to schematics," Thomas says. "Then we'll put the funding plan in place and see what it will take to make this happen. It's long overdue. We need to get up to speed and get the project done."

Air conditioning, club boxes, luxury boxes, loges, more restrooms and additional concession spots are among the items on the plan. No work will start, Thomas said, until "we have 80 percent of the funding model in place." A part of that money will come from corporate or private sources that have an interest in the premium amenities that will be available.

But Thomas is an advocate of maintaining the Assembly Hall, rather than tearing it down and starting anew. "Most of those conversations [for closing the Assembly Hall] were prior to my arrival," Thomas says. "In our situation, the Assembly Hall has iconic status and we don't want to be in position of it going away completely. . . . If the building were not iconic in nature, and with a great foundation, I might have a different feeling. People in this state have warm and fuzzy feelings about it, as they should.

"It's outdated in so many ways, doesn't give the home-court advantage you seek and doesn't have all the amenities you want, but the condition ... the University and the DIA have done a wonderful job of maintaining it."

Fans shouldn't expect overnight changes. "It will probably happen in stages," Thomas says. "We could get it done sooner, but then the men's and women's games would be off-campus and we're not excited about doing that. Two years is a reasonable time span [to complete work]. We won't disrupt a basketball season."

Ideally, work could begin in the summer of 2013, which would give a target date to finish renovation in time for the 2015-16 season.

"People have an affinity for that building," Thomas says. "It won't look significantly different [on the outside]. It will still have the spaceship look, but there are things to do with the exterior glass. That's how we'll extend the concourse. We want the building to have that 'wow' factor."

As for the inside, Thomas's hope is "we don't shrink the capacity too much," although the configuration will be altered. With the court-side seating, he says, "the plan is to get it tighter to the floor and make it more of a home court advantage."

Groce advocates the plan to keep home games intact. "If it makes the process a little longer, I support that decision," he says. "I agree with the decision to keep all the home games in the Assembly Hall."

Former Illini Dave Downey is among those pleased that the building will remain intact and in use. "I don't think it needs to be replaced," Downey said. "It stood the test of time better than I thought it would. It still looks as good as anybody else's [facility]. The fact that we have a great record there doesn't seem to hurt our recruiting." Since leaving Huff Gym for the Assembly Hall, the Illini men have won more than 75 percent of their home games. They played their 700th game at the Assembly Hall during the Big Ten portion of the 2012-13 season.

Groce likes what the building is, and what it represents. He's also anxious to see what it can become. "We have some work to do, in terms of moving forward," he says. "It's a great building to begin with, but now we have a chance to improve and grow its vast 50-year tradition. . . . I'm very excited."

The established tradition of excellence, which has led to a cumulative UI home record of 542-145 (before the 2012-13 season), will not be diminished.

"It's a great home-court advantage," says former Illini Bill Small, who is a still regular attendee at games. "They don't dare tear that thing down, but it amazes me to think they'll spend more than $150 million to renovate it."

Some of those dollars could come with naming rights for a corporation or an individual. But whatever it is named, it almost surely will still be "the Assembly Hall" to most — albeit with a facelift to host another half-century of memories.

Thanks for the Memories

"What's the best game ever at the UI Assembly Hall?"

This is one question that can never be answered with certainty. It might be the one when a last-second shot secured a win for the home team, or one which produced a milestone victory for the coach. It might be one that clinched a championship or landed the Illini in the NCAA tournament. It might be one of the Chicago Bulls' eight exhibition games (1970, 1974, 1976, 1977, 1978, 1989, 2008 and 2012), or one of the more than 250 high school state tournament games contested before the IHSA relocated the boys' and girls' events.

Perhaps it's the one where a father and son watched the action in person together for the first time. Maybe it's the one where a fledgling sportswriter witnessed his first game in the facility. It might be the one where a future star first ran out of the tunnel and into the spotlight.

It could even be one of the four games Michael Jordan watched as a spectator when his son, Jeff, was a member of the Illini. The games were certainly memorable for the fans lucky enough to get an autograph.

The point is clear. There are a myriad of significant games and they can vary according to who is creating the list. None is really more important than another if they remain vivid in the viewer's mind long after the outcome was determined.

What is Your Favorite Memory of the Assembly Hall? The community responds:

The time we saw Billy Graham . . . New Year's Eve. — Philippe R. Jacques

The very first memory I have of the Assembly Hall is when I was about 4 or 5 years old and my mom took me to see "Sesame Street Live." It was so amazing and I loved it. My favorites where Bert and Ernie and I can remember when they sang the "What a Name" song and they said my name. Great memory. I hope that someday I will get to take my little boy to see something like that at the Assembly Hall. — Michelle Burris

I remember getting to the Assembly Hall early for the Steve Martin show. I was hanging out with my sister and listening to what was happening on stage. We heard the most amazing banjo music. It wasn't until later that we realized that it was actually Steve Martin playing. — Kathy

I have a few different favorite memories of Assembly Hall. I saw my first collegiate basketball game there (Illini vs. Minnesota), which was a great experience. I experienced some of the best concerts I've seen there in Jimmy Eat World and O.A.R. I met Lewis Black, one of my absolute favorite comedians, there (and enjoyed his stand-up set as well, of course). I set my personal best for a 5K at the Illinois Marathon, which starts right next to Assembly Hall. It's a place that will always hold a strong place in my memories. — Anthony DiPietro

In March 1963, I traveled to Champaign for the Illinois High School Basketball Championship held in the brand new Assembly Hall. At the time I was a junior at Lanphier High School in Springfield, and bus loads of kids came to support the Lions who ultimately won third in state. I remember being blown away by the size and beauty of the Assembly Hall. It made such an impression. I can still remember exactly where we sat (in B behind the Illinois bench). Everytime I go to an Illinois basketball game, I think back to my first visit to the Assembly Hall. What an experience! — Peter Tracy

Flooding the court as part of the Orange Krsuh after upsetting Michigan State on College Gameday, February 2010!
— Paige Millburg

[I have] scores of good memories of sports and concerts, but the earliest memory is going to the circus and riding an elephant outside the of the Hall. — Richard Bobowski

He-Man and Masters of the Universe (He-Man chased Skelator around the access railways at the top of the Assembly Hall. When you're little, that's SUPER cool. WWF Wrestling Hulk Hogan/Ultimate Warrior/Honkey Tonk Man. — Jeremy Larson

Being there December 1, 2004. Illinois vs. #1 Wake Forest. Illinois thoroughly destroying the #1 team in the country and setting the stage for the most memorable basketball season in recent memory. NEVER heard the Assembly Hall louder than that day, it was truly a special night to have been in attendance! — Eric Bramowicz

Standing in line for over 8 hours, wrapped around parking lots clear back to First St., to see the president of the United States at that time, Bill Clinton. It was a once in a lifetime opportunity and well worth the wait. The Hall was packed. — Chalaine Davis

Garth Brooks! — Allison Darsham

The biennial National Order of the Arrow Conference [Boy Scouts of America] took place August 23-25, 1963, at the University of Illinois Assembly Hall. — Steve L. Hettinger

I have a several good memories. First, seeing my late cousin, a U of I student, perform in the Music Man when I was 4 yrs. old. It was magical. Being stuck at home in a blizzard as my folks were with Chet Atkins, Floyd Cramer, and Boots Randolf at the Assembly Hall. The first date I had with a now late boyfriend listening to Jackson Browne. Nearly falling asleep at the end of an eventful prom weekend with Chuck Mangione. Sitting behind the stage for Huey Lewis and not minding because of the view. George Strait shaking my hand at his performance when my husband was deployed. George had a cold and I just knew I'd have lots of explaining to do to my husband. And spending our first wedding anniversary with the Moody Blues. Other outstanding concerts in my mind were Charlie Daniels, Journey, Manheim Steamroller, Kenny Rogers and Dottie West. — Jackie Joines

When I was a junior in high school, I was fortunate enough to be a reserve on the Effingham High School basketball team that played in the Elite Eight in March of 81. Uwe Blab was our center, and we dressed in the Illini locker room. I used Perry Range's locker. Coach Jim Maxedon told us that would be an experience we would remember the rest of our lives, and was he ever right. During introductions, I tripped stepping up onto the raised floor of the Hall and nearly face planted in front of several thousand people. In December of 2011 the Effingham teams of 79-80 and 80-81 had a 30 year reunion that refreshed a lot of those memories. That was a great time in many of our lives. — Tim (Stewart) Onstott

My aunt, Mary Claire Smith, worked for the Assembly Hall most of her working career, beginning about a year before its doors opened. She was Tom Parkinson's administrative assistant, then Wayne Hecht's.... One of her most cherished memories was shortly before she retired, the circus was booked and she got to ride in on an elephant and was honorary ringmaster. She was thrilled to step out from behind the scenes! — Michael Smith

Seeing Bob Hope, Bill Cosby, etc. (1960's). Also first Illini basketball game in building. As with thousands of others, Champaign H.S. graduation held in the building. — Bruce Prestin

As a third-generation Illini, the Assembly Hall has been host to a number of significant and joyous events in my life, from my participating in the Illinois State Science Fair to great concerts from groups like Chicago to exciting Illinois basketball games (chanting "Lou-Lou-Lou") to my own graduation ceremony in 1981. It has remained an inspirational architectural icon. — Chris Carpenter

My favorite memory is my first concert ever. I was 8 years old and got to see Lee Greenwood, Dolly Parton and Kenny Rogers in concert. It was so awsome! Sitting outside the Assembly Hall for 2 days to get 4th row tickets to see New Kids on the Block! That was like having a slumber party with 200 people — it was a blast! Being in the 1st row at a Kenny Chesney concert and getting autographs! My best memory is graduating in 1993 from Urbana High School in the Assembly Hall. — Angela Lus

All the fantastic concerts in the 70s: Grateful Dead, Jethro Tull, Emerson, Lake & Palmer, etc. They just don't do concerts like they used to! — Patty Smith

I must have been 3-4 years old and my parents took me to the circus at the Assembly Hall. This is actually my earliest childhood memory. — Brandy Harness

1979, Illini vs. Michigan State. Eddie Johnson hits buzzer beater for the win! I recall that Governor Thompson was in the building that evening and a bomb threat was phoned in before the game. An announcement was made indicating that everyone was free to leave due to the threat. No one moved. The prevailing sentiment in our section was that if it was our time to go, the Assembly Hall was a great place for it! — Judy Ferber

1. Eddie Johnson buzzer beater vs. MSU
2. U2 concert in 1987. — Andy Hoggatt

My wife and I took our two daughters to their very first Illini game on December 12th, 2010. We braved one of the worst winter storms in years to get to the game from Peoria. When we got there it was mentioned that it may have been the lowest attendance at the Hall even though it was sold out. The four off us, with our big orange fingers, had one half of the C section to ourselves. Everyone else migrated down to the lower levels. We stayed put so the girls could be as loud as they wanted without disturbing the others. To end the night, Paul Klee came up and interviewed us for the paper. It was at that moment that I realized how stupid and dangerous the trip from Peoria was, but the girls loved it and talk about it today. We made it home alive, while many others ended up in the ditches. — John Love, Jr.

1. Being part of the first graduating class at the Hall in 1963.
2. Broadcasting Eddie Johnson's famous winning shot against #1 Michigan State.
3. Attending the Elvis Presley performance — the crowd was as much to see as Elvis was.
4. Directing Bob Hope to the nearest restroom as he and his entourage arrived at the Hall for one of the first shows there.
— Dave Shaul

My parents brought me to Champaign to the Assembly Hall for the first time, to see the Ice Capades with Sesame Street characters. I thought they were taking me to the alien ship and it was going to fly away with me, so I was completely terrified. I vaguely remember having to be carried into the building kicking and wailing. Then I saw the Sesame Street characters, who were definitely not aliens intending to eat me. So I loved the show to bits. But I still didn't want to look back at the building as we were leaving, just in case the aliens had been hiding…. — Dena Strong

My father, James Bradley, worked for the U of I out of the physical plant as a painter and retired from there. The Assembly Hall will forever be a part of my memories because dad helped paint the top of the Hall at least twice while a painter for the U of I. Somewhere was a photo of him on top abd I remember he was just a dot. — Rhonda Bradley

Def Leppard "In the Round" in C-U
Many great rock 'n' roll acts have played the Assembly Hall, and one of them was Def Leppard on Oct. 16, 1988. It was a place and time in music history, the apex of "hair metal" mania, and the sold-out crowd was pumped up to a level that I've never witnessed at any concert since. The band's gigantic, colorful stage and dazzling light show were par for the course at the time. Singer Joe Elliott boldly roamed the stage, touching on subjects not meant for young ears; and during the concert's final moments, one-armed drummer Rick Allen, who looked unhealthily pale, stood next to guitarist Steve Clark, who would be dead in less than three years. Both musicians fully looked the part of traveling rock stars who rarely see daylight, which made the show all the more enthralling to my 15-year-old eyes. It was hands down the best concert I've ever been to, and I've seen lots of great ones. — Sal Nudo

The Rolling Stones concert in 1969. I was able to get great seats on the floor. When the Stones came on stage, I was one of the first fans to run up to the stage and position myself right in front of Mick Jagger and Keith Richards. I remember Mick asking Keith between songs "Where are we, anyhow?" Answer: Assembly Hall in Champaign, Illinois! — Edward Green

In the late 1970s and early 1980s I was a huge REO Speedwagon fan. It wasn't until 1983 that I was able to see the band at the Assembly Hall. Since then I have seen them three other times at the Hall. The last time I saw them at the Hall was in 2009, and I had floor seats. I brought my then 12-year-old daughter to the concert with me. She and I were able to work our way to the front of the stage and got some handshakes and guitar picks from the band members. It only took me 29 years to get to the front of the stage at an REO Speedwagon show! — Cindy Webb

I have 2. The first one was when Dwayne Schintzius from Florida was pounded by tennis balls during player introductions. The second was a nationally televised game with Oklahoma and Wayman Tisdale. Illini was up by 1 with like 8 seconds left. Oklahoma was in bounding the ball right in front of me. Efrem Winters tipped the in bounds pass. Anthony Welch caught the ball in lane and hammered it home to put the game out of reach. Needless to say, the Hall exploded. Awesome experience. — Tim Weikle

My dad took me to the first basketball game. It's been 50 years and I still have my ticket stub and program. More important, I have the memory that my dad and I did something special. I've attended concerts (I met Garth Brooks after a sound check — Lou Henson was with us), I've seen historic basketball, but nothing comes close to being that 10-year-old boy sitting next to his dad watching the Illini play in "The Saucer" on a foggy March night. — Dan Swaney

When my mom and dad were able to get B section seats to the sold out Elvis Presley concert in 1977. It turned out to be one of his last shows. — Cindy Steck

My favorite memory of the Assembly Hall was my mother. She was an employee of the Assembly Hall for 26 years before she passed away. It was a very important part of her life and she was quite proud to work there. — Mark Williams

As an Illini Alum (LAS Class of '70) and the Assistant Basketball Coach of the Joliet West Lady Tigers, in 1978 I had the dream experience of being in the Illini locker room, walking the cavernous tunnel, treading on the sacred Illini court, sitting on the sideline experiencing the same hopes and anxieties of all the Illini coaches and appreciating all the cheers and accolades from the fans as the Lady Tigers received the Illinois State Championship Trophy on a late Saturday evening in February. Sweet! — Constance A. Kozikowski

I will always remember seeing my first Reba McEntire concert in the Hall. It was amazing! I did not realize until that evening in February of 1995 that this arena was so versatile. Reba was driven onto the stage by a taxi cab! A real taxi cab! Unbeliveable! — Darren Talbott

I coached a "game" in the Assembly Hall in the early 1990s! I talked the Athletic Association into letting me hold a scrimmage for my Urbana Park District youth basketball team during halftime of a UI women's game. My oldest son Sam coached one team. I coached the other. It was a real thrill to hear our names called out over the PA system as head coaches. My youngest son Zack (probably age 10 at the time) hit a three point shot during that game! He caught a pass, looked down at the floor, stepped behind the three point line, and drained a shot! — Bernie Sloan

I regularly attended UI women's basketball games in the Assembly Hall (late 1980s and early 1990s). Attendance was pretty sparse. You could easily get a front row seat if you got there early enough. One time [at a women's basketball game] my name was called to participate in a halftime contest. Hit one of two free throws and win a free Blimpie's sub sandwich. I thought it was a sure thing. But as I stepped up to the free throw line I noticed that several members of the men's Flyin' Illini team were seated right behind the basket. I think I remember Steve Bardo, Nick Anderson, and Kendall Gill. They were rooting for me! I choked under the pressure, and my first shot was a brick, but at least I hit the rim. Before I took my second shot, one of them yelled "C'mon, you can do it!" My second shot was a perfect swish, and those Flyin' Illini were cheering me for a shot I had made on the Assembly Hall floor. Very surreal! — BG Sloan

My favorite memory would have to be the Kenny Rogers concert back in the early 80s. It was my first time in the Hall and I was amazed at how everything worked so smoothly. It was a building to be reckoned with. Later I was thrilled to usher at the Illini ball games. Thanks to the U of I for having the vision to build it. — Cliff Wilson

I saw Bob Hope do his stand up comedy show there in the mid-1960s. The Mills Brothers were the opening act. — Ed   Porter

After watching the Milwaukee Bucks play, my family and I were leaving and outside we saw Lew Alcindor (Kareem Abdul-Jabbar) sitting in a car. I asked him for his autograph and he got out the car and all I could do was look up. As a young kid that is a moment I will never forget. — Camilla Smith

I was a senior in high school and came to CU for a campus visit. A freshman friend of mine from Lockport, IL, acquired two tickets for the UCLA and Illinois game, very good seats at that. The Illini, with Brody, Thoren, Redmon and others, took down John Wooden and the NCAA championship team from the prior year. That sealed the deal, I enrolled the following fall. — Joe O'Brien

I had a good friend that worked in the office that booked shows at the Assembly Hall. At dinner one night, she said, very quietly "Guess what . . . Elvis is coming to the Assembly Hall." I lost it and let out a small scream. Then she added, "You must not tell anyone because it is still a secret." She not only trusted me with that secret, but she also got me tickets to the show for my birthday. That was the first and only time that I had the best seats in the Hall and will never forget the performance that Elvis delivered that night. My friend is gone now but the memory of her trust in me and the gift of the show will never be gone. Yes the night will live always in my memories and my heart. — Ellen Fondren

I was 10 years old in the early sixties. Our family had recently moved into Paxton from a nearby farm. My mother signed me up with a church group to travel to Champaign to see the Ice Capades at the newly opened Assembly Hall.
I had seen newspaper photos of the ongoing construction of the Hall, which was the talk of the area. But nothing could have prepared me for that first visit. Walking toward the Hall from the parking lot, I felt like Dorothy approaching Emerald City. A gigantic spaceship had landed and I was granted access to its dazzling interior where acrobatic aliens were gliding on perfect ice that shimmered in a kaleidoscope of colors. The Ice Capades show was a delight, but for this young boy, the star of the show was the stunning venue. I have been to hundreds of games and events at the Hall since that day, but none compares to that first trip. — Tony Lee

I was going to Piper High School and came to Champaign as a 4-H summer camp delegate. Our family had hosted an IFYE guest, Maria from South America. My petrifying task was to introduce her from the floor of the Assembly Hall to the several hundreds attending. — Patricia Gallahue

When our daughter Cindy Arthur, who was a girls basketball coach at Bushnell/Prairie City, brought her team to the Assembly Hall to play in the Girls Championship Games. They ended up winning 3rd place. It was such an exciting and great time. It was considered such an honor to get to play at the Assembly Hall. On two other occasions we were at the Assembly hall and have memories of bringing our grandchildren to see the Harlem Globetrotters and when a granddaughter graduated from college there. — Kay & Myron Shonkwiler

When I was 9 years old, my dad took us out to the Assembly Hall construction site and took home movies of us walking about with the skeleton of the arena in the background. A few months later, we attended the Open House and I watched Les Paul and Mary Ford on the stage while marveling at the incredible interior of the arena. Then later, in the mid 60s, I was at the David vs. Goliath Pekin-Cobden IHSA Championship game. My first concert was Loggins and Messina in the early 70s. Then I came to work there in 1980 as the Event Manager. Cultural and life milestones have been marked at the Assembly Hall over the last 50 years for me and many others. I am still in the sports and entertainment business, due in no small part to the Assembly Hall. — John Graham